THE HUNDRED OF DEVONPORT

D1529487

A "Hundred" is a medieval term for a division within a county.

In 1848, in order to control the use of "wastelands" or Crown Land, the Crown formed the six Hundreds of the County of Eden. Along with Takapuna, Devonport was included in the Hundred of Pupuke. The Hundred was dissolved in 1854.

The Hundred of Devonport

A Centennial History

Edited by S. Musgrove

A panoramic view of Devonport taken from Rangitoto, 9 November 1900.
Auckland Public Library

First published in 1986 by
the Devonport Borough Council,
  Victoria Road,
  Devonport,
  New Zealand.

ISBN 0 908704 06 2

A Shoal Bay Press production
Cover design by Chris Pearson
Typeset by Glenfield Graphics Ltd
Printed in Hong Kong
Distributed by Benton Press, Box 33-055, Takapuna

Contents

It is always important for all communities to look ahead and to plan for the future of the citizens, but it is also necessary to look back once in a while. A centenary provides just such an opportunity to review what has been achieved and to pay tribute to the contributions of predecessors.

Devonport has a double reason to celebrate the centenary of the Borough. It was one of the pioneer communities of New Zealand and it has been the home of the Royal New Zealand Navy. In both cases it has played a very significant part in the development of New Zealand.

I hope that the citizens of Devonport will feel proud of their heritage and that it will encourage them to work even harder for the future of their Borough.

1985

Acknowledgements

The Devonport Borough Council would like to express its appreciation to each of the contributors and the editor, Professor Sydney Musgrove. This appreciation extends to the Centennial Sub-committee of Council, chaired by Councillor Kelvin Grant; the Council staff; the centennial co-ordinators, Richard Tong and Georgina Morrow; and the working editors David Elworthy and Ros Henry. The photographic research was undertaken by Julie Benjamin and the contemporary photographs were taken by Chris Miller. Council would like to express its appreciation to the *Auckland Star* for making their photographic facilities available. The co-operation of many individuals in supplying photographs from their family collections is gratefully acknowledged, as is the generosity of the following institutions in authorising the reproduction of photographs held in their collections:

The Alexander Turnbull Library
Auckland Institute and Museum
Auckland Public Library
Auckland Star
Devonport School
Devonport Museum
The National Museum
The New Zealand Herald
North Shore Times Advertiser
Pegasus Press
Royal New Zealand Navy
St Paul's Presbyterian Church

The following companies have contributed donations to the Centennial fund which has assisted in the production of this volume:

Frank Allen's Tyre Services
H.J. Asmuss and Company Ltd
J. Bigelow Ltd
Gulf Mazda Ltd
Hornsby Earthmovers Ltd

R.F. and J.A. Renouf
J.G. Sharp and Son Ltd
Strangs Bookshop Ltd
Worley Consultants Ltd

Introduction

This book is not a definitive history of Devonport — such a history has yet to be written. Instead it is a celebration of the local community which provides a series of images of our recent past. Anyone reflecting on his or her own past will appreciate that the very recounting of historical events can distort and confuse the actual reality, but this publication has, I hope, painted a faithful history of the Devonport Borough.

The individual contributors, most of whom are Devonport residents, have evoked between them a lively picture of our small community, which although so typical of New Zealand, is also splendidly unique.

To all past and present elected members and staff, and the residents and ratepayers who supported them, I hope this volume inspires continued pride.

W.D. Titchener
MAYOR

Eruera Maihi Patuone, a Ngapuhi chief, elder brother of Tamati Waka Nene.
Patuone died in Devonport in 1872. *Alexander Turnbull Library*

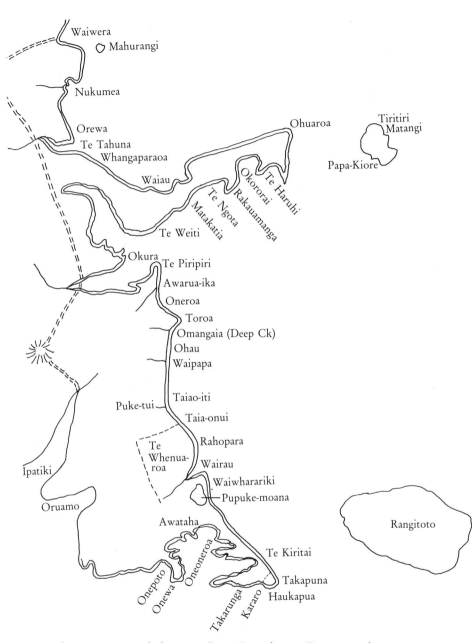

A map of Devonport and the East Coast Bays in pre-European times.

The Beginnings

David Simmons

This land of Aotearoa was a thing fished up by Maui and this island is Te Ika roa a Maui (the long fish of Maui). The custodian of that fish was Kui and his people Ngati Kui grew up on Maui's fish. They dwelt here for many years, then another people migrated here from beyond the deep. Their name was Tutumaio. Having landed here on Te Ika a Maui they began at once to fight with weapons and craftiness. They also intermarried with the people of Kui, both the men and women. When their wars were finished the people of Kui had disappeared. They had gone down under the earth to live. So Te Ika a Maui was taken by Tutumaio.

For many years Tutumaio held Te Ika a Maui then a party sailed here from beyond the deep. Turehu was their name. They had hardly arrived and come ashore at Te Ika a Maui when warfare began between the Tutumaio and the Turehu. It was a warfare of weapons and craftiness. There was intermarriage between the men and women of either party, the one with the other, and the Tutumaio became extinct. The possession of the land was passed to the Turehu.

For many years the Turehu dwelt in Te Ika a Maui, when there again came a party from beyond the deep, descendants of Maui, looking for the fish of their ancestor. Maori was the name of the men who settled down in Te Ika a Maui. They fought with weapons and also fought with craftiness, did the Maori with the Turehu and they intermarried, the men with the women, the one with the other. And so disappeared the Turehu. Their issue grew and multiplied in numbers and the possession of Te Ika a Maui passed to their descendants. Forty-six generations of the Maori have been dwelling in Te Ika a Maui.

Now, listen, O people of this land. Consider Kui, Tutumaio, and Turehu, who have disappeared. None of them is left to answer the repeated calls.

As for Tutumaio, he reappears as an apparition in the sight of the eyes; before long, it disappears. As for Turehu, his reappearance is as Patupaiarehe who goes out above on the mountains, speaking. Just as a man is its speech, not like a spirit is the speech of Turehu. Now all together have disappeared, these people and their craftiness. It is always thus with craftiness.

This is also the craftiness which leads astray, beyond the pathway of their god Io o nga manu. They leave their going astray as a cause of anger of Io to that people, and thus there is left only Tapua (monsters) as a curse upon Te Ika a Maui. For, they have sinned against their very mother's milk. They have lit cooking fires to cook their mother, and have eaten the fat and flesh of their mother, and so her fat and flesh have turned upon them, so they have disappeared!

This tradition was recorded in 1890 by George Graham from Wiripo Potene, who died in 1905 at the age of ninety-four. Potene was a member of the Kawerau tribe which formerly owned the whole of the offshore islands and the coast from Takapuna (North Head) to Mahurangi.

In 1856 Edward Shortland published an account of Tainui written by Tamati Ngapora, a close relative of Potatau Te Wherowhero, the first King of Waikato. According to this story, the first landing made by the Tainui canoe was at Whangaparaoa, where the canoe was held fast by rock oysters. It sailed from there to Te Apunga o Tainui (the billow of Tainui) at Otahuhu where it was portaged across to the Manukau Harbour. In other versions of the story related by Hoani Nahe of Ngati Maru to John White and recounted in Volume IV of *The Ancient History of the Maori*, Tainui did not go across the portage but went around North Cape.

Tainui is not the only canoe associated with the area, according to Te Ao of Arawa in Shortland's *Maori Religion and Mythology*. The string of islands from Cape Colville to Whangarei are known as Nga Poito o Te Kupenga o Taramainuku (fishing islands of Taramainuku's net). He was the grandson of Tama Te Kapua, captain of the Arawa canoe, who lived for a time at Moehau then later settled in the Kaipara. Another settler of Arawa descent was Tahawhakatiki, the son of Hei, the elder brother of Tama Te Kapua. He settled at Whangaparaoa.

The Kawerau, who arrived later, recognised the Tainui but claimed true descent from the Rangimata canoe under Marupuku. Another canoe from which Kawerau takes some origin is Te Wakatuwhenua, the canoe which landed at Kawau, nearly all the people on which died from leprosy. This is also the origin of the people who lived

Patuone's grave on Mt Victoria. *Auckland Star*

further north at Te Arai, the Ngai Tahuhu. Ngai Tahuhu seem to have been a branch of Kawerau and like them were closely related to Ngati Awa who are traditionally said to have migrated from Northland to establish themselves in Taranaki and in the Bay of Plenty.

Kawerau originally held all the land between the Weiti River, Mahurangi down to the Manukau, as well as the Waitemata at Takapuna (North Head). After 1650 their territory was reduced by the Ngati Whatua conquest. The Kawerau were left in occupation at Long Bay, Torbay, and other areas of the coast, even though they owed homage to Ngati Whatua. In the late eighteenth century, raiders of the Ngati Paoa of the Hauraki Gulf took over the offshore islands and ventured between Rangitoto and the coast using the Awanui a Peretu (the channel of Peretu), now known as Rangitoto channel, to attack the Kawerau along the coast. The Ngai Tahuhu tribe protected themselves by giving a chief's daughter in marriage and exchanging a greenstone mere. Some years later, Ngati Paoa themselves used the same mere as a gift to make peace with the Ngapuhi musket raiders at Panmure. It didn't work and the Ngapuhi even used the mere later as an excuse to attack the Kawerau and Ngai Tahuhu.

The last chief of Kawerau was Te Rangikaketu, whose grandson Hetaraka laid claim to the whole of the Auckland area. The boundaries of Rangikaketu's land were from Takapuna (North Head) to beyond Orewa and then inland.

In 1841 the Mahurangi Block from Takapuna to Te Arai was purchased. The sellers were the chiefs and people of the Kawerau, Ngati Whatua, Ngati Paoa, Ngati Whaunaunga and the Murutuaha tribes of Hauraki. The last two groups of tribes were the more recent conquerors of the area. Some descendants of Kawerau still live in East Coast Bays, where their earliest ancestors probably settled about a thousand years ago.

Early Stanley Bay (Brick Bay) c.1890. *Lackland photo*

The Island Borough

John Morton

The early inhabitants of Devonport used to call it "The Island". They had good geological reason, for within living memory Devonport was almost an island, with only the tendon of Narrow Neck tying it to Takapuna.

Indeed before the Auckland eruptions of 40,000 years ago it was probably not one island, but three—a large mass of cliffed Waitemata papa, twenty-five million years old, extending from Vauxhall to Stanley Bay; and two small off-liers, the cliff block making up the present Fort Cautley and Stanley Point beyond the present spit. Shoal Bay at that time formed a stream flowing into the Waitemata River, and a tributary out of Ngataringa Bay had eroded Narrow Neck to a thin divide on the outer side of which the cliffs were being attacked by waves, without the shelter which Rangitoto offers today.

Then came Auckland's eruptive phase with the formation of three volcanic cones—North Head, Victoria and Cambria. Spreads of tuff, scoria and alluvium soon linked them to the older papa cliffs to give Devonport Peninsula its present shape. But to the turn of the century Ngataringa Bay still stretched right up the Narrow Neck sandspit, and in north-easterlies caught the spray from Rangitoto Channel.

The first of the volcanoes to appear was North Head, a tuff cone with a crater filled with scoria which spilled over its rim and buried it. Next came a fire-fountain with a vent near Vauxhall, which formed the attractive little scoria cone, Mt Cambria, and probably others too, like Duder's Hill, once visible near the waterfront. Last to arrive was the scoria cone of Mt Victoria, whose summit crater was breached to the south-east and poured out the basalt flow which today extends to the shoreline. Devonport's present business area is sited on a boulder bank in the lee of Mt Victoria.

During this volcanic period the sea level was also rising as the glaciers melted, and the cliffs exposed to the north-easterlies were steadily eroded back at North Head. The highest sea level was attained perhaps 3,500 years ago. Thereafter North Head was joined to main Devonport by a sandspit across the open gap at Cheltenham. Stanley Point became attached by its own narrow spit, while at Narrow Neck yet another sandspit probably closed the connexion between the Ngataringa salt marsh and the open sea.

Devonport had thus been constituted in almost its modern shape when the Maoris first arrived to occupy the spaces between the hills,

Some examples of Devonport's cliffed Waitemata papa, twenty-five million years old. *National Museum*

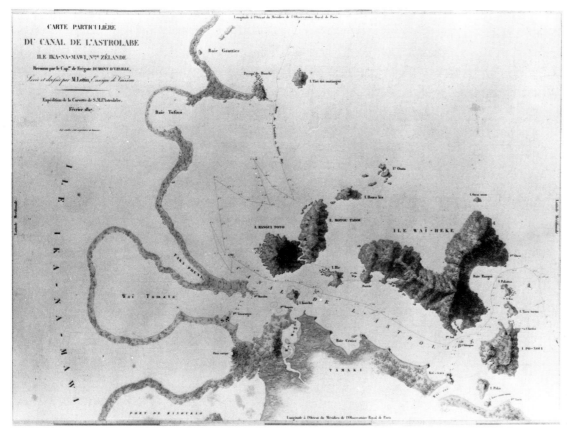

Auckland Harbour, from a chart prepared by Dumont D'Urville, and published as part of an atlas entitled *Autour du Monde* in 1827.
Alexander Turnbull Library

and to terrace and fortify the fine bush-clad heights. Tradition says that the Tainui canoe landed at Whangaparaoa, but on attempting the entry to the Waitemata Harbour became stranded on a sand-bank east of the present ferry wharf. Here the leader Taikehu swam ashore.

Centuries later, in 1827, the first Europeans were to make the same landing. From d'Urville's exploration ship *Astrolabe* the surveyor Lottin was the first white man to climb North Head. A survey station was established on Mt Victoria, and from Mt Eden too, the new-comers gazed across the wide expanse of the Waitemata, the isthmus and the Manukau. In 1884, Lieutenant Godfrey, surgeon of HMS *Urgent*, sketched the three cones with their original vegetation. The same scene still appears in Hoyte's romantic harbour-scape of the sixties.

North Head was once resplendently crowned with pohutukawas coming right down to the shore. Griselinia, karaka, kohekohe, ngaio and mahoe grew there too, with Prince of Wales feathers and clematis on ledges and crags. Mt Victoria was clad with fern and spear-leafed mountain flax, amid the varied greens of bracken and manuka. Secure and watchful, the Maoris had then lived among the hills where d'Urville first looked out on the gulf—the Shoorakai of the new colonists, or Ooahaouragee to Captain Cook.

The view is just the same today.

Mt Cambria (*left*) and Mt Victoria (*right*) in 1899. This photograph was taken from Old Lake Road, and shows the Takapuna Racecourse in the mid-ground. *Paul Titchener collection*

THE HAND OF MAN

Colonial man soon laid a commanding hand upon the North Shore, and has been its dominant species ever since. The tale is still one of ecology, with an aggressive and ingenious species in charge, though not always a ravager and a polluter.

Some places have been effaced or altered beyond recognition. All the fine bush from the hills is gone, pohutukawas replaced by dry summer grass, or fringes of privet, pine and macrocapa; but the

panorama from the top is still superb. One volcanic cone, the thirty-metre high Mt Cambria (the "Hill of Sheep") has, like little Duder's Hill, been totally quarried away. Its scar, once the Borough depot, has been transformed into a promising shingle garden.

Devonport's most landlocked coast, the mangrove swamp where Ngataringa Bay reached over to Narrow Neck, was filled in just before the turn of the century to make the Takapuna Racecourse, today

Alison Park. A new direct road to "The Lake" has replaced the Old Lake Road (still signposted) that found its circuitous way from Vauxhall through Narrow Neck. Ngataringa's old expanse of salt marsh and shore plants is almost lost, like nearly all such habitats in metropolitan Auckland. A fine avenue of pohutukawas and Norfolk pines is there today instead. Cheltenham had once a rich and diverse tidal flat. Above the shore its panoramic beauty is still there, with tree-lined streets and verandahed villas, in the quiet of a week-long Sunday afternoon. The beach is still interesting too, but its finest living shells of forty years ago—*Alcithoe* and *Struthiolaria*—are no longer there, probably owing to pollution from stormwater run-off contaminated by Devonport's antique sewage system.

Before the threat to Ngataringa Bay in the 1970s, the navy had already filched large bits of it in reclamations. The significant little sandspit which joined Stanley Point to the main has been blocked in its line of view by a disastrously placed public toilet, but up to its present bay-head Ngataringa still has good coastal walks, where banded rail are to be seen, as Shoal Bay has red-breasted dotterel. South of Stanley Bay there are high papa cliffs, weathered back to leave an intertidal platform, diversely rich in marine life.

The North Head walk is of a quite different character, narrow and full of incident, with a scramble of garden escapes—periwinkle, nasturtium, star of Bethelehem, amidst bright lantana and yellow heads of fennel.

These changes chronicled, we have listed the worst. Much remains to redeem the damage of the recent past, with a Devonport enhanced and recreated by the happenings of a hundred years.

Top right: Stanley Point in 1890, with the full tide visible on both sides of the neck. *Lackland photo*

Bottom right: The papa cliffs of Stanley Point, c.1890. *Keiser family*

THE VICTORIAN LANDSCAPE

When building has happened finely or gracefully, it has generally been without benefit of town and country planning. This need not be true in future. From the Devonport of last century there is a treasury of glass-plate negatives to show what a distinction the little borough had, with its gardens, orchards and paddocks cut up by stone or paling fences; old streets and lanes, with cottages and verandahed villas, shingle-roofed and with chimneys that are fine examples of the bricklayer's art. There were some two-storeyed homes too, modestly affluent, while most of the Devonport dynasties, Niccol, Mays, Duder and the rest, were already established around the Flagstaff.

The picture we have is of a secluded cross-harbour Remuera, at a time when that eastern suburb too was made up of the villa-scattered fields and lanes which Hoyte and Kinder have recorded. The townscape became concentrated up the slope of Victoria Road, a street that never fell into the dowdy decline of Ponsonby, nor yet aspired to the up-market frivolity of today's Parnell.

In its nineteenth century houses and public buildings, Devonport had a style altogether unpremeditated, which neither here nor in Auckland at large was to be achieved again. The designs assort well with each other because they are graceful and artless, seldom architectured, most perhaps originating from the plain, reliable taste of the builder's copybook. These were young days when Devonport was building better than she knew ... and all with "the great unconscious gravity of a girl".

Devonport has come down to us as a condominium of scattered styles and moods. There is the little Grey Lynn, barer of trees than the rest, that slopes down to the bay behind Hastings Street and Melrose. Calliope Road is a Ponsonby, with its less affluent side contrasting with its more spacious harbour-facing slope. Beyond the

Top: Looking west from Mt Victoria in 1909, showing Stanley Point in the centre and the districts of Melrose and Sunnyside. *Auckland Public Library*
Bottom: A view of Stanley Point and Ngataringa Bay in 1926. *Auckland Public Library*

isthmus of the bay, the change is striking. Stanley Point has its mansions in North American grandiose style, set back on sections rich with trees. It has the same apartness and social isolation as Herne Bay with its old pohutukawas and the drop of cliffs at the water's edge.

How different is the waterfront of King Edward Parade, full of weekend goings-on: with the neighbourhood "pub" of the boating world at the Masonic; new resorts like the Bakery and the glassworks and curious shops; and in front its forest of masts and spars, and the hauling-out ramps of Duder's Bay.

The oldest, most secluded streets are those that run up, steep and narrow, from the parade towards Mt Victoria. Mays Street, Church Street, St Aubyn Street, all have old houses, high-gabled and balconied, now coming into new life with intensified "unit" development. These are still not out of harmony with the over-run gardens behind shaded walls, and what was the old power station standing in Mays Street since 1914.

Further east, and somewhat like a maritime Mt Eden, are the favoured slopes where Takuranga Road runs to the base of North Head with its plentitude of good houses and richness of trees—puriri, karaka, tree-tulip, Moreton Bay fig and camphor laurel.

Looking east from Mt Victoria in 1904. *Auckland Public Library*

Taken on the same day, this view looks south-east from Mt Victoria across the harbour. *Auckland Public Library*

The Esplanade Hotel and Victoria Rd, looking from Victoria wharf, c.1935. *Devonport School Album*

Devonport's high tide of elegance is at the foot of Victoria Road where the esplanade commands the seafront, worthy—save for its modern beer-hall—to rank with the stucco of England's Brighton or Eastbourne. From the beginning of Devonport time, the ferry wharf has stood here, grandly roofed and enclosed since 1926. No longer throbbing with morning and 5 o'clock crowds, it is today tatty and forlorn. For the first thirty years, the small naval establishment stood where Windsor Reserve is now. The narrow beach—like Cheltenham —was then a fashionable promenade, with closed-off salt water baths, and its small, well-architected changing shed out in front.

Victoria Road is still Auckland's best suburban street. Its shops and two-storeyed facades in concrete wash, white stone or Suffolk pine, columned or verandahed, nearly all date back for a century. They have a harmony of mood and scale, with a whole world of difference from Takapuna's neurotic jangle in Hurstmere Road. One or two gaps have broken the fine sequence. The worst is the ugly plate-glass front, substituted for the arches and columns, of the old Auckland Savings Bank, a treasure which the Trustees should have cared enough about to save.

Two Devonport views taken in 1923. *Left:* Looking south-west from North Head towards Auckland and Mt Victoria. *Above:* Looking north-west towards Narrow Neck from North Head. *Auckland Public Library*
Below: The former ASB Building in Victoria Road, demolished in 1965. *Paul Titchener collection*

DETERMINANTS OF TODAY

If Devonport, like Sydney's Balmain, is a virtual island with its front approached by sea, it has never been beyond sight or intrusion from the city. The 1950s brought the heaviest incursion: these were the scarified years when queues of commuters in cars inflicted on themselves and on Devonport delays, discomfort and pollution that by 1959 were no longer tolerable.

It was then that the harbour bridge diverted traffic suddenly through Northcote. It also brought to an end overnight something that for a century had been uniquely formative of Devonport's character, the daily confraternity of the passenger ferry.

The first regular ferries crossed the harbour early in the 1860s, by sail or rowing boat at sixpence a trip. The first, ill-fated little steam ferry *Emu* was lost in 1860. The seventies began a long, picturesque era of steam. The ferry crossing was an unhurried microcosm of the life of Devonport itself, an instalment of leisure which no commuter today would imagine it possible to enjoy.

Until the turn of the century there were the paddle steamers, broad-beamed like crinolines, out of the building yards of Niccol, Logan and Bailey. Small at first, like the *Tongariro* and *Tainui*, they were followed by the great names of the eighties, *Victoria*, *Alexandra*, *Eagle*, *Brittania* and *Osprey*, commissioned by the ambitious house of Alison.

With the new century came the twin-screw propellor-driven ferries. The oldest of us will recall the last days of the odd, two-funnel-abreast *Condor* built in 1902, and in successive guises pioneer vehicular ferry, up-harbour excursion boat, and high-built Noah's Ark. Her successors on the Devonport run were the *Kestrel*, *Ngoiro*, *Peregrine*, *Makora* and *Toroa*. Three vehicular ferries ran to Devonport, first the little *Goshawk* (1909) then the *Mollyhawk* and *Eaglehawk*. After the war came the single diesel-propelled *Korea*; but the diesel age was to be cut short by the bridge.

The Ngoiro, c.1930. Lackland photo

Marine Square and Victoria wharf entrance, c.1930, with E.W. Alison Memorial and clock to the left. *Mrs M.J. Walters*

Twice daily the ferry wharf used to hum with crowds, to and from the line-up of yellow buses. A couple of small brown buses served Cheltenham and Vauxhall which years before had boasted their own tramway.

Each hour of the ferry day was different. After the early morning workers' runs, business from eight to nine crowded the upper cabin, the outside decks or the narrow cabin downstairs. Through the long afternoon, the two musicians played on board, and at five the crowds appeared again. The last ferry at night drew the tired or romantic souls away from the Ferry Building's colonnades, with the moon on the water, or the white surge around the moorings.

Through it all sounded the throb of engines, with thrusting rods and polished brasswork, the smell of oil and the hissed escape of steam. There was the frenzy of the bell, and the hurried reversal of the screws, then the thud of the gangway, the whining of tight hawsers and the rattle of deck chains.

PROSPECT FAIR

All of Devonport's history, with its pulses of engagement and withdrawal from Auckland, has taught it certain things about local government. Different from the city, and even from the bustling remainder of the Shore, the Borough now has some 10,410 souls on 578 ha of land and with sixteen km of coastline.

After the loss of the ferry traffic in 1959, and the Borough's threatened contraction overnight, Devonport was uncertain about what it wanted to be—whether, under such terms, it wanted to revert to its traditional detachment.

The Ngataringa Bay development proposal is covered in a later chapter. The final decision was made by a community that had time to reflect upon itself, and make a conscious decision on what it aspired to become ... or continue to be. Twenty years ago and less, municipal talk was confident of amalgamations. Devonport would be merged eventually and inevitably with the younger and larger city of Takapuna, fast-expanding and with just a few of its forgotten corners as beautiful as the small borough to its south.

Today's assumptions are different. Community Councils, with their traditional and identified locality, may have an influential role to play. The old borough could then become the new "community". Whatever kind of larger structure might be superimposed to handle regional matters, Devonport would seem, in the vision of Henry May's Local Government Act of 1974, just what a "community" was meant to be. With its community council, but with the continued dignity of Borough, and its elected Councillors and Mayor, Devonport could be pre-eminently of the right size to go on governing itself, and determining its essential character.

The ferries in pre-bridge days.
Top: Passengers leap the gap between deck and wharf as a ferry ties up at Bayswater in 1946.
Bottom: The *Mollyhawk* photographed from the harbour bridge just before the service ceased in 1959. *New Zealand Herald*

Local government, since the Ngataringa battle, has found itself able to tap new resources among Devonport people. Particularly has a new style developed in town planning. Decisions have been seen to become more democratic, argued out with good citizen rapport, often upon the local site.

The scheme for the recycling of domestic refuse at the old gasworks site has set an imaginative example for New Zealand. Here is something larger municipalities have tried and failed to get started, while Devonport was a community just large enough to bring off.

Devonport's independence is still equivocal and interesting, as it relates to Auckland beyond. The Borough has a high proportion of professional—including academic—people, both commuting and retired. It has patently its own character, a little idiosyncratic. But it has few of the resources—business, commercial and financial—to be able to withdraw into itself, as might Takapuna in some measure. This could also be culturally true. Significantly, Devonport has never acquired its own secondary school.

Still, we may predict that much of Devonport's future will be determined indigenously and at home. History tells us of the "lamp-post" beside the Esplanade Hotel, where at the turn of the century knotty civic problems used to be argued out. To some of its people today, it is not hard to sense within Devonport a new pulse of citizen involvement. Like some old-style commune, assembled on a fine Sunday morning on Windsor Reserve, at the Cricket Ground, or on the commanding slopes of North Head, we could imagine it as a little Swiss democracy, in its own town meeting, ready to contemplate its present self, and its century ahead.

The Esplanade Hotel. Many knotty civic problems have been argued out beneath the elegant lamp-post on the left. *Auckland Institute and Museum*

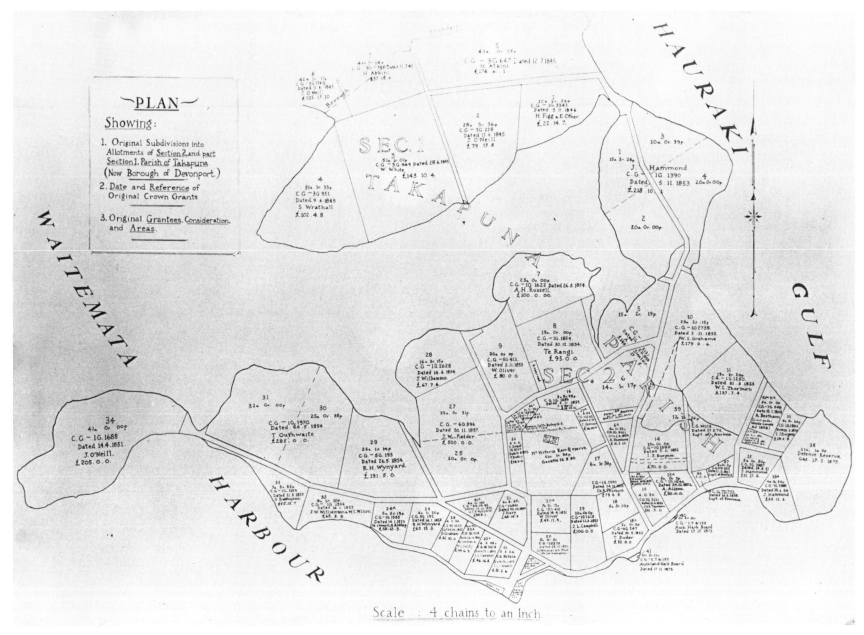

Original sub-division of the Borough of Devonport.

The Borough

Gael Ferguson

Five hundred rats were killed in Devonport in June 1901. For many years previously the Borough Council had also had to contend with the problem of dead dogs washed up on the beaches. The rats were not peculiar to Devonport. Their death, and the recording of their numbers, were the results of a nationwide campaign—"Rat Week"—conducted by the Government. From time to time there had been fears in settled areas of bubonic plague, scarlet fever, and other infectious diseases. There was a growing awareness of the problem of public health and sanitation. The Council's participation in "Rat Week" is merely representative of any small community's development and "institutionalisation". The problem of the dead dogs is another matter. These were unique, because of the harbour's tides and Devonport's position on the peninsula, which made difficulties for the Council. The need to dispose of the carcasses was a fact often recorded in Council minutes.

But dead dogs are not the only examples of Devonport's idiosyncracies. These include the Council's sometimes odd adminis-tration of Rangitoto Island, Ngataringa Bay, the presence of the army and the navy, Cheltenham Beach, Cheltenham School for Girls, the decades of foul water supply, the ferries, the shipbuilders, the Chinese Gardens, the Strawberry Gardens, Bear Gardens, Vauxhall Gardens, C.C. Dacre, Oliver Mays, Edward Bartley and Ewen Alison's wall.

This essay offers a brief and somewhat attenuated survey of Devonport's past, concentrating on two periods, 1850-1900 and 1960-1984. The years between are not neglected, but I believe that the earlier and later periods are of particular importance. The earlier time was one of development, of the growth of a community, and has a vitality which seems missing during the next fifty years. From 1900 to 1960 Devonport was merely consolidating its early development and, more importantly, coping with the massive problems of depression and war. Perhaps these two events explain the plodding nature of the borough's existence—at the Council level at least. They did, however, have the effect of revealing a community vulnerable to change and certainly sensitive to any change in its image.

The heritage of war and depression was a society which believed in development and physical change to the environment. Frequently it was development without sensitivity, and in Devonport's case the period after 1960 was a time of fervid pursuit of such a goal. The responses to these pressures for change are important to Devonport's present character. Through such programmes as the rubbish recycling system and such apparently minor matters as changes in attitude towards building controls, Devonport could offer to the "outside world" a different view of what should constitute the urban environment. The recent past should not be neglected for what may seem the more romantic time of a hundred years ago.

Devonport, until the 1860s known as Flagstaff after the signalling station on Mt Victoria, was purchased from the Ngati Paoa as part of the Mahurangi block in 1840-41. (Final settlement of ownership was not completed until 1854.) For a decade the area was occupied by only a small group of families associated with the naval stores and ammunition depot established below Elizabeth House in 1841, and the signal station which was set up in 1842. During this period the area was in the hands of the Crown, which in 1848, in order to control the use of "waste lands" or Crown land, formed the six Hundreds of the County of Eden. Along with Takapuna, Devonport was included in the Hundred of Pupuke.

Local settlers were given some control of their affairs through the wardens of the Hundreds, who administered the licensing of grazing on common land. The first Devonport licence-holders were P. McLaren, farmer, Henry Figg who leased land near Woodall Park, and Thomas Duder, who had come to Devonport in 1843 as Signalmaster.

The first signs that the settlers wanted independence from the wider Hundred came early in 1853. At one meeting people objected to the conducting of the election of wardens, but more importantly, and indicative of the growth of the area, it was pointed out: "that there was not then sufficient unsold Crown land to justify the issuing of depasturing licences for cattle which were depastured practically on the private property of other cattle owners", which was unjustifiable under any circumstances. At another meeting in March 1853 the settlers pushed for three separate areas—Flagstaff, Shoal Bay and Stokes Point and the provision of a ferry service by the Provincial Council. They emphasised that in order to withstand moves for a northern road from Stoke's Point that "the main road from the beach on the North Shore, near the Flagstaff and thence to Maurice Kelly's at the Wade opens more of the country and of the best land ... is the shortest (and the cheapest) of any road that would be laid down"! Nothing came of this particular meeting, and in 1854 the Hundred was dissolved by the simple act of the Wardens declaring the waste lands outside the Hundred and giving themselves nothing to administer. For the next thirteen years they were governed directly by the Provincial Council.

The collapse of the Hundred is noteworthy, for it signals the beginnings of Devonport's development into a residential borough. The cause of the collapse was the sudden increase in population due to the subdivision and sale of Crown land as suburban farms in 1853. The new arrivals were not satisfied with the existing administration, but they also wished to ensure that the land in which they had invested was enhanced by making Flagstaff the centre of any transport route north. The names that appear at this time became dominant in Devonport's later administration and were the forerunners of several local "dynasties", some of whom still survive. Thomas Duder, James Hammond and William Oliver had all arrived before 1853 but in that year the names of Alex Alison, Thomas Hammond, T.M. Bartley, and I. Burgess also appear.

The actual subdivision of Devonport into suburban farms occurred in 1850. At this time many of the main roads, albeit paper ones, were formed. This, with the retention of certain parts of the area by the Provincial Council, is probably the most significant event of the decade, apart from the actual arrival of settlers. King Edward Parade and Queen's Parade (originally known as Beach Road) were surveyed, as were Victoria Road, Church Street, Cheltenham Road, Albert

Mt Cambria, now long quarried away, with Cheltenham in the background, and Vauxhall Rd leading diagonally across the centre. *Burton Bros. c.1880-85. Christine Turner*

Street, Clarence Street and Calliope Road. The names of course were devised later. Similarly the subdivision of lots dictated later roading as different landowners subdivided and sold their land. Thus Duder's Avenue lies between the sections owned by Thomas Duder and Alex Alison. Certain areas of land were retained for public use although their status at the time of the formation of the borough was to be a vexed question for the Council. Nevertheless their exclusion from sale is the basis of Devonport's existing system of reserves; it also encouraged the continuing presence of the navy within the borough.

The Superintendent of the Province retained the land which was later to become Devonport Domain. North Head was a defence reserve, gazetted in 1878. The navy owned the Triangle (that area on which the library now stands) and what later became known as Windsor Reserve. A metal reserve was retained on Mt Cambria lying between what became known as Vauxhall Road and Church Street. Mt Victoria was kept by the Crown for many years, although in 1880 it was gazetted as a recreation reserve to be administered by the Mt Victoria Domain Board. The Auckland Harbour Board owned two small areas along King Edward Parade, below Duder's Hill and on Torpedo Bay.

By 1854 there were fifteen Anglican families living in and around Devonport—sufficient to petition Bishop Selwyn for aid in forming a school. But despite this initial settlement the period when Devonport began to take on the sense of being a separate community was in the 1860s with the arrival of the shipbuilders. Alex Alison had been involved in boat-building since 1853, but between 1860 and 1880 Devonport was probably the biggest ship-building centre in New Zealand. Some initiatives had been taken earlier of course—a parish school was formed in 1856—but it was in 1861 with the arrival of Oliver Mays as schoolmaster that the three of the four groups that made up early Devonport had arrived. The fourth group was the military, who, although there had been a volunteer coastguard unit stationed there since 1860, did not truly arrive until the 1880s.

The three earlier groups were the settlers, the shipbuilders and people like Oliver Mays (schoolteacher, shopkeeper and postmaster) who provided services to the rest of the community. These three were to be a powerful force long after the population had been swelled by newcomers in the 1880s and 1890s. By 1867 the Flagstaff District Highways Board was formed; George Webster, Henry Niccol, Frederick Woodhouse, George Beddoes and James Hammond were elected. These men were to share power for the next fifty years with, among others, Thomas Duder, Malcolm Niccol, William H. Brown, Robert Duder, James Mays, Ewen Alison, Edward Burgess, Philip Mason, William Philcox, William Bond, Robert Wynyard, Joseph Macky, Charles Dacre, William Philsen, Robert Logan, Samuel Cochrane, William Cobley, James Holmes and Edward Bartley. The latter was to leave a lasting impression with the buildings he designed for the borough.

The close relationships between these early men and their connexions with local politics did not always prevent conflict. Oliver Mays seems to have disliked the shipbuilders and Malcolm Niccol in particular, who actually ran a chandlery rather than built boats.

VOTING PAPER.

BOROUGH OF DEVONPORT.

Names of Candidates for Election to the Office of Mayor. November 26th, 1890·

ALISON, EWEN WILLIAM.  *157*

MAYS, OLIVER. *117*

N.B.—The Voter must draw a line through the name of each Candidate for whom he desires NOT to Vote.

He must leave only ONE (1) Name un-cancelled, or the Voting Paper will be invalid.

He must fold the paper so as to conceal the contents, and put it into the Ballot Box without allowing the contents to be seen.

4 informal votes

The battle for the mayoralty, 1890.

"Map of a portion of Northfleet, now called Devonport ..." Undated. *Auckland Public Library*

He also fought constantly with Ewen Alison and through his membership of the Waitemata County Council and the Harbour Board was frequently at odds with the Council. Mays carried his dislike through to Niccol's and Alison's protegés in local government and frequently obstructed such important schemes as provision of a water supply. The rivalries of the 1880s and 1890s were to be continued well into the twentieth century and were probably partially responsible for some of the Council's later actions.

Some did quite well out of their relationships with local politics. James Mays and the Duder brothers, as local contractors, benefited from the pressure to install a comprehensive drainage system and in particular to build roads in the borough. Others such as Ewen Alison seem to have enjoyed a fight with the authorities for the sake of it. While actually sitting on the Council, E.W. Alison was taken to court for alleged encroachment on Beach Road. He won and eventually cost the Council £800.

Interest in local politics and pressure for a local administration came from an increasing awareness of the possibilities of development in Devonport and the need to provide services. During the 1860s there was considerable speculation in land subdivision, although the large-sale development occurred in the 1870s and 1880s. The "Village of Devonport" at the foot of Mount Victoria was advertised in 1859, the North Devonport estate, the "Township of North Cheltenham" in 1864, George Beddoes' land at Cheltenham, and the Holmes Brothers' six allotments of "North Fleet" on Victoria Road in 1865. Almost all of these subivisions were based on speculation about the formation of a viable ferry service.

The Flagstaff District Highways Board, later known as the Devonport Roads Board, was formed as a direct result of this speculation. Their first act in 1867 was to institute a roading programme, including ... "upgrading the road near the Masonic Hotel, upgrading Sheep Mount (Mt Cambria, which was later quarried away), and upgrading near Vauxhall Gardens" (originally owned by William Cobley). In 1870 work was begun on the formation of Beach Road and by 1872 the Board was considering laying iron.

We are not sure of the identity of the paddle steamer, but L.H. Cobley is standing at the end of the gangway on Victoria Wharf with W. Jenkins of the Devonport Steam Ferry Co. Captain George Emirali stands on the paddle cover. 1880s. *Auckland Star*

A constable was appointed in 1869 but because the Board was unable to bear the cost he was replaced in 1873 by a special armed constable paid for by Government. In 1876 after a case of typhoid fever was reported the Board resolved to request proclamation as a Local Board of Health which gave it increased control over all sorts of nuisance. In 1878 a free library was opened (the first in the Provincial district) and in 1883 fourteen gas lamps were brought to Devonport. Their placement gives an idea of the most established areas in the borough:

"Beach Road on the corner of Anne Street, on the Triangle opposite the Post Office Store, under the willows by W.H. Fenton's, the corner just above Rattray Street, Flagstaff Corner near the gasworks, the triangle near the Holy Trinity, the corner opposite Duder's, and Beach Road corner near Grey Street (Mays Street)."

The 1880s began another period of growth. The army arrived in force and proceeded to construct defence works on North Head. The Devonport Steam Ferry Company triumphed over all others. City

Alison's strawberry gardens on Beach Rd, run by Roderick Alison. *Dr A. Armitage*

businessmen were beginning to settle in the area and a number of large residences were constructed. "Sunnyside" subdivision was advertised, as a result of speculation on the effects of the proposed Calliope Docks. Devonport was becoming the commercial centre of the North Shore, and Victoria Road was sufficiently important commercially for the Council to pass protective ordinances requiring brick walls between shops after a particularly devastating fire.

Over the next twenty years Devonport began to develop as a "marine suburb", residential in nature and an important recreation area for Aucklanders. While farming was still important (or more correctly, gardening and the supply of food even to the extent of providing the city with daily milk and cream) there was a decline in small holdings. The development of Alison's strawberry gardens and the provision of strawberry teas for Sunday visitors was to be as important an activity to Devonport as any farming or even industry. Clerks, book-keepers, bank officials who worked in the city commonly became residents.

For a brief period before the economic collapse of the late 1880s a number of "gentlemen of independent means" resided in the borough. Builders of course were highly necessary tradesmen, and the ever-resourceful Duder brothers added this to their long list of enterprises. George Quick began his Bear Gardens and the *Waitemata Messenger*, a weekly paper which began in June 1885, transferred to Devonport in 1896. For women there was some chance of work they could pursue. Taking advantage of the more affluent population milliners, dressmakers, tailoresses and machinists set up. In 1890 a music teacher and a woman accountant lived and worked in Devonport, while in 1900 could be found a bookbinder, nurses, telephonists, a photographer and an artistic frame-finisher.

Beside such developments the gazetting of the Devonport Borough Council in 1886 is of little real significance. Such an administrative change is after all merely the recognition of population growth. Generally the Council was a continuation by the same people of the same work as had gone before, but in one area they did begin in grand style. In 1889 they persuaded the Harbour Board to take responsibility for the dead dogs for a time, and they began to grapple with the problem of reserves and parks. The borough was unusual in that at its incorporation it had very few endowments of land for reserves. In 1870 the Highways Board had petitioned the Commissioner of Crown Lands to allow ratepayers to use Government land. They were refused. Three years later Mt Victoria was offered to the Board for recreational use—Thomas Duder was grazing cattle on it at the time. A public meeting was called to organise a planting campaign, the Board having just received £50 for that purpose from the Provincial Treasurer. However in 1878 the Board was roundly snubbed when the jurisdiction of North Head was given to the Waitemata City Council—Devonport's arch enemy. Possibly as a result of this, the Council donated £1 to a petition to abolish the County Council in

1880. In 1883 the Highways Board acquired the scoria reserve on Mt Cambria, ensuring the ultimate disappearance of the mountain. In 1884 the Board was given the right to use the navy Triangle.

Thus by 1886 the Council had the right to use the reserves but did not own them. The first action of the Council was to have their jurisdiction extended to mean low-water mark—the reason being that the paper road along the waterfront was below the high-water mark and would have been exempt from Council's provisions. In 1890 the borough acquired twenty-one acres of cemetery reserve, Cheltenham Beach to low tide, the public school reserve and two small portions of Mt Victoria. In the same year Rangitoto Island was bought under the Public Reserves Act and the Governor's powers delegated to the Council as the Rangitoto Island Domain Board. The Board was to come under considerable criticism for its administration—for allowing baches, for instituting Arbor Days when groups planted exotic plants on the island, and for beginning quarrying. In 1890 the Council obtained twenty-two acres of reclaimed land at Narrow Neck from the Harbour Board.

The Council's desire to acquire the Triangle and the Sandspit (Windsor Reserve) was dictated partly by the fact that they had built Council Chambers (designed by Edward Bartley) there illegally. Their panic over the chambers had important ramifications. In 1890 a letter was sent to the Governor asking that the Admiral leave the Council Chambers on the Triangle. The local MP replied ... "I feel conciliatory approach to the Admiralty from time to time will prevent inconvenience ever happening re removal of offices." There had been pressure for a large squadron to be located at Calliope Dock and it appeared that the Admiralty were willing to sacrifice much to have it happen. E.W. Alison, Mayor at the time, replied to the MP ... "recognising the importance of conciliating authorities Council will coincide with proposed arrangements but propose moving that the Harbour Board offer the Admiralty land adjoining Calliope Dock with deepwater frontage in exchange for the Government's promise to help in consequence of their offices being on the Admiralty reserve."

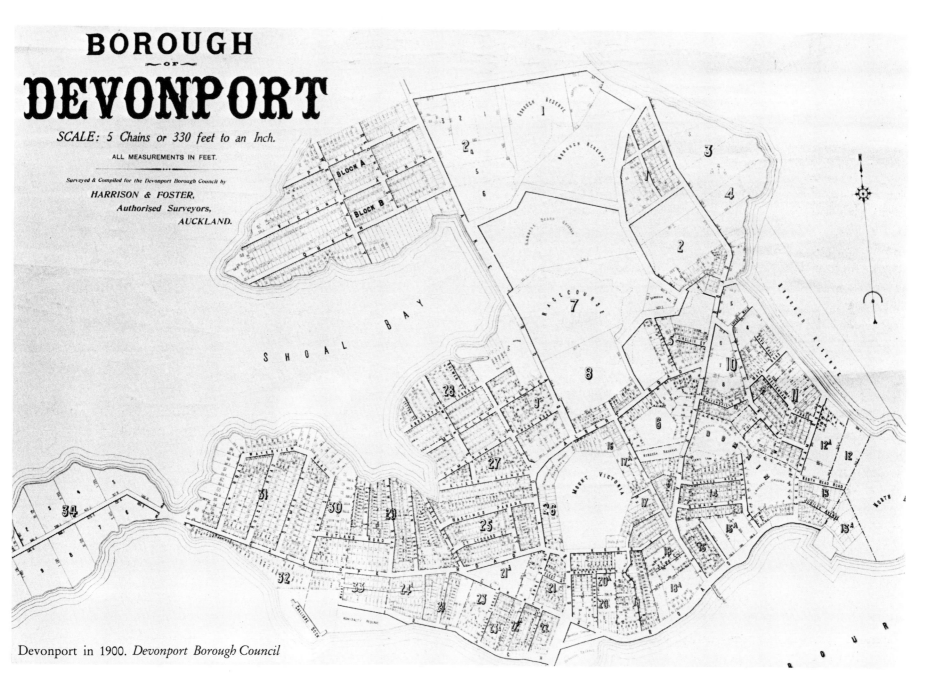

BOROUGH
~ OF ~
# DEVONPORT

SCALE: 5 Chains or 330 feet to an Inch.

ALL MEASUREMENTS IN FEET.

Surveyed & Compiled for the Devonport Borough Council by

HARRISON & FOSTER,

Authorised Surveyors,

AUCKLAND.

Devonport in 1900. *Devonport Borough Council*

"The Laird of Lochaber". The Hon. E.W. Alison
Auckland Institute and Museum

Malcolm Niccol, Mayor of Devonport, in Grand
Mason's regalia. *Joyce Keely*

This portrait of Oliver Mays appeared in *New Zealand Graphic* 2 May 1903. *Auckland Institute and Museum*

In the end the Harbour Board obtained the reserves in exchange for four acres at Calliope Dock—at the time of negotiations Malcolm Niccol was Mayor of Devonport and Chairman of the Harbour Board. An Act of Parliament in 1894 gave Devonport the Triangle, and Windsor Reserve was exchanged for five acres of land at Narrow Neck. In many ways the cost to the council was high—land lost to the Harbour Board and, more importantly, sufficient land to encourage the establishment of the naval station meant the presence of the navy has been a powerful influence ever since.

The next fifty years of Devonport's history (1900-1950) is essentially one of consolidation and "coping". True, the Council from time to time toyed with grandiose schemes for town halls and public baths. Edward Bartley, a long-serving councillor who had been responsible for designing many of the larger buildings in Devonport, provided a number of elaborate drawings for future town halls. The Council became enmeshed in questions of electricity supply, water supply, trams, rates, maintenance of roads and other practical problems of the times.

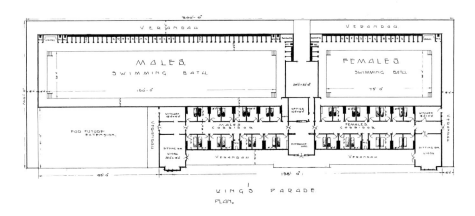

Edward Bartley, the architect of many of Devonport's finer buildings, including Holy Trinity Church (1885) and its vicarage (1887). *Devonport Borough Council*

Bartley's elegant proposed borough council chambers, were, alas, never constructed. Nor were his proposed swimming baths which exhibited a clear prejudice in favour of the male. *Devonport Borough Council*

The greatest scandal of the period was the water supply. Originally Devonport was supplied by a series of wells and rainwater. An aquifer running the length of Church Street was tapped, and in some cases examples of wells still remain—on Tudor Street, next to the old Devonport Electricity Supply building where the bagwash used to be, and near Cambria Road. William Cobley sank two wells opposite the Masonic Hotel—one for the use of the town and one for the ferries. During the 1890s Ewen Alison as Mayor instituted a pumped supply from Lake Pupuke. By the 1910s it was apparent that the supply would be inadequate and in 1922 the Public Health Department issued a warning against using the lake supply. The whole issue of finding alternative water was tangled with the issue of metropolitan supply, and political rivalries between Mayor Lamont and Council hindered action. Devonport vacillated between finding its own supply and joining a metropolitan scheme, and at one time considered a private supply from the Waikato. Still nothing was done, and by 1940 the water was putrid—thousands of dead eels and fish were found in the badly polluted Lake Pupuke and the Council was buying 5,000 gallons a day from the Auckland City Council. Even the old wells were brought back into use. Devonport eventually joined the metropolitan supply.

HOW TO FILL A KETTLE IN DEVONPORT.

Water problems refused to go away.

Above: There was no shortage when the Lake Pupuke water supply was opened on 11 August 1894. *Devonport School Album*

Above right: But half a century later there were dreadful problems, and water had to be supplied by tank. *Paul Titchener collection*

Minhinnick also had some strong things to say and draw about the Pupuke water supply as early as 1933. *The Herald*

SPEAKING OF THIS NORTH SHORE WATER SUPPLY, THE SUPER-CHLORINATION IDEA IS LIABLE TO CAUSE SOME TROUBLE —

HAVEN'T YOU HEARD? POOR OLD JIM HAS UNDERGONE A SERIOUS OPERATION — HE HAD TO GO TO A BUILDER'S YARD TO GET HIS BOILERS CHIPPED!

1933, MARCH.

OF COURSE, SOMEBODY ELSE MIGHT LIKE THE STUFF. — LET'S CAN IT AND WORK UP A BIG EXPORT TRADE —

YES, MADAM, — GENUINE TAKAPUNA SOUP MADE FROM FRESH NEW ZEALAND TAKAPUNAS — A KIND OF SHELL FISH, I UNDERSTAND !

FRESH SHIPMENT IT'S TAKAPUNA SOUP

PERHAPS IT'S GOT A MEDICINAL VALUE —

TRY OUR PUPUKE LOTION REMOVES WARTS, HARES MOSQUITOES & MOTHERS-IN-LAW

CHEMIST

ANYHOW, IF IT'S GOING TO COST SUCH A LOT TO INSTAL WAITAKERE WATER, WHY NOT INSTAL SOMETHING MORE ORIGINAL WHILE WE'RE ON THE JOB —

JOHN! OSCAR'S BEEN DRINKING HIS BATH WATER AGAIN! HE'S THROWN ALL HIS SCHOOL BOOKS AT ME AND NOW HE'S STANDING ON HIS BED SINGING 'THE RED FLAG'!

STRONG DRINK

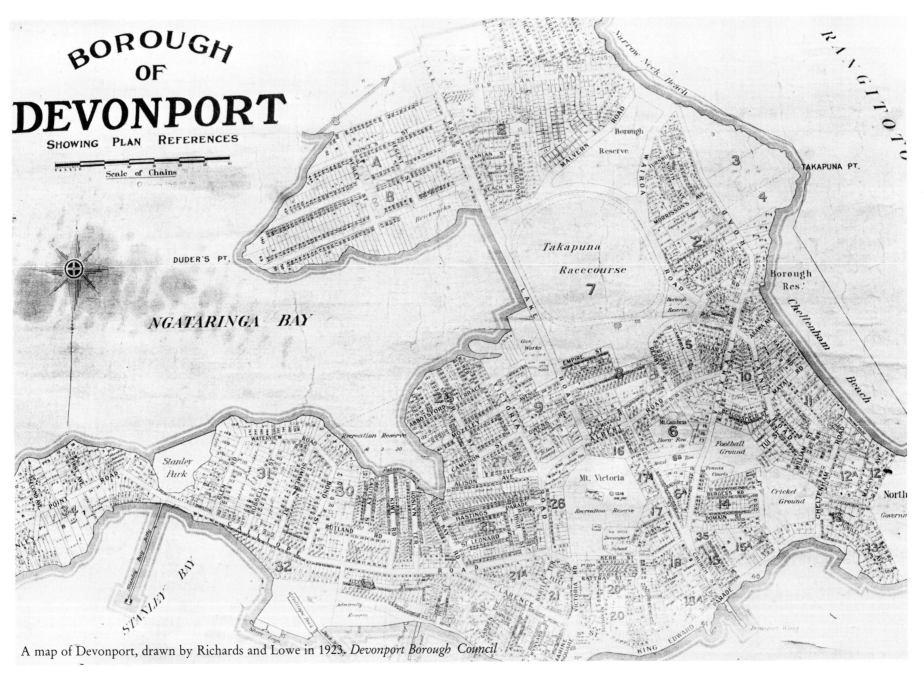

A map of Devonport, drawn by Richards and Lowe in 1923. *Devonport Borough Council*

The fifty-year period was one of dealing with massive "outside" disasters—war and depression. For the latter the conduct of the Council was similar to its counterparts elsewhere in the country. It sought and received unemployment loans for work schemes, while retrenching, dismissing employees, cutting rates and supporting various welfare agencies for the unemployed. The first application for a loan was made in 1926 in order to extend Queen's Parade by 100 feet. In 1928 £12,000 was received from the Government, but the money was spent on little of lasting benefit. Melrose Park was begun, Mt Victoria cemetery was cleared of weeds, and a committee for the relief of the unemployed was set up. Interestingly one of the demands to Government was that schemes be applicable to both sexes, an unusual request in the light of the general neglect of unemployed women.

Labour camps had been set up in Takapuna, but in 1934 the Government planned to move the men to work on Hobsonville air base. The Council objected, insisting that the men be found work closer to home. It also defended twenty-five Devonport men who left the Hobsonville scheme. Despite the Council's advocacy the local unemployed were far from happy with its administration of relief programmes, and in 1933 a number of them backed their own candidate, T.P. Gilfedder, who was secretary of the Welfare Association, for Council elections. He was unsuccessful. By September 1933 the Council was supporting 174 relief workers with supplies of wood, vegetables, meat and boots from a welfare depot set up in the old powerhouse.

The unemployed left few of their own records in Devonport apart from those works in which they were engaged; most information available comes from the point of view of those who administered relief funds. Perhaps the most telling record is in the exposure of the poor state of housing in the borough after the depression.

The new 1935 Labour Government conducted a nationwide survey. Of 2,816 dwellings surveyed in Devonport 134 were overcrowded, mainly around Calliope and Vauxhall Roads. Twenty-three per cent were found to be unsatisfactory but repairable (apparently a high figure), 57 per cent were in a satisfactory condition while 4 per cent

John A. Lee opens the first state house in Devonport on 26 September 1938. *Auckland Star*

were unfit for habitation. The Government chose to place some of its early state houses in Devonport—in the northern area which was still in pasture, and a favourite place for blackberrying. Thirty-five sections were purchased and forty-six units built, despite objections to state housing from some councillors.

Before the community could really begin to take stock of the housing problem war was declared. Aside from the personal tragedies and difficulties the practical impact of the war was a compound of trivia and irritation. Devonport's case was more extreme because of its position on the peninsula and the presence of the navy. Barbed wire was taken off the beaches later than elsewhere, and the blackout stayed in force longer. By 1942 600 slit trenches had been dug in the borough and the Council was sufficiently organised to take records of next-of-kin of soldiers departing overseas. Confusion seems to have reigned in other matters, and the women of Devonport were forced to call a meeting to try to resolve issues such as the provision of air-raid shelters and evacuation plans. Various groups organised themselves to provide comforts for the departing troops, many of whom passed through Devonport.

The War served to entrench the navy even more in the borough, a fact resented by many who objected to large areas of land being made available for their use. However the extra buildings that the military had occupied on Mt Victoria proved useful. These were converted into transit housing with some reluctance by the Council and at the prompting of central Government. Applications for the housing revealed substandard conditions in Devonport, particularly at Narrow Neck.

A popular view of Devonport is that the construction of the harbour bridge in the late 1950s caused a sudden and rapid decline in the borough's fortunes. That it dealt a body blow to the residents' image of the settlement as a "marine suburb", or as a thriving commercial community central to the transportation of goods north is true. However, the struggle of the Council to provide services, and the often appalling conditions of the 1920s, 1930s and 1940s reveals a community which had already begun to decline from the heady days of the 1890s. The affluence of the older families was not a sham, but it masked a community which obtained its living from very ordinary occupations and basic shop-keeping services. Devonport might have been the beginning of the road north, but nobody stopped there; the vehicular ferries gave the place a spurious air of activity.

Some of the strange decisions of the next few decades were not caused entirely by the trauma of becoming a backwater. They were representative of the general spirit of the age which saw physical development as the answer to its problems. Devonport's inhabitants voted in a series of Councils who were convinced that the future lay in developing or redeveloping the borough. It was to be a return to the vitality of the 1870s and 1880s, but unfortunately Devonport had little to "sell", and it gradually became evident that there was a growing body of citizens who did not wish to "sell" anything at all to the wider world. Ngataringa Bay of course was the climax of the period—it was the most grandiose, and potentially the costliest scheme of all.

The first intimation of change came in 1948 with the demolition of the old Bartley-designed band rotunda on Windsor Reserve, and moves by the Devonport Businessmen's Association to raise money for a soundshell to be built there. Four years later the ratepayers rejected a loan proposal for £229,600 for roading improvements. Following this rejection the Council seemed to turn away from its customary role of providing small-scale improvements to the borough and instead began to be actively involved in major development proposals. The harbour bridge debate was raging at the time and the Council was caught between those who welcomed the idea as a means to rid themselves of the traffic congestion and others who saw it as death to the borough. In early 1950 Mayor J.R. Miller had favoured a tunnel to Devonport, but by November such views had been overtaken by events and the Harbour Bridge Bill was passed on 1 December 1950. After that the Council could only protest at their lack of representation on the Bridge Authority.

Air raid shelters can be quite fun as long as the war is thousands of miles away. *Alexander Turnbull Library*

Detachment of No. 1 Territorial Special Force Reserve at gunnery practice, North Head, in November 1937. *W.L. Ruffell collection*

A New Zealand Coastal Defences searchlight crew at practice in 1940. *Photo: A.W. Breckon. Alexander Turnbull Library*

During the 1950s there was no attempt at concerted policy. For instance, in 1951 the Council opposed attempts to have an international airport sited in Shoal Bay but in December 1955 decided to urge the Auckland Harbour Board to reclaim 300 acres of Ngataringa Bay. Little came of such plans at this stage but meanwhile the Council had got its teeth into the idea of redeveloping the cityside waterfront. The Auckland Metropolitan Planning Organisation had been pushing the idea since 1947; they had a vision of multi-unit high-rise development on the slopes of Mt Victoria which would house up to 10,000 people. In 1957 the Council proceeded to sell some houses it owned on Devonport Domain and called for tenders for high-rise development.

It was typical of Council decisions during this period that they actually tried to sell before finding out whether they had the power to build on a reserve. In 1962 they were still arguing the case with the Commissioner of Crown Lands, who insisted that the Council had to prove the land unsuitable for recreation before it could be taken for high-rise development. In September 1964 they investigated proposals for three twelve-storey blocks of flats comprising 100 units on the waterfront at Torpedo Bay. Their proposal to use land vested in the Devonport Mt Victoria Domain Board was refused outright by the Minister of Lands in April 1965. The results of these sorties into high-rise development was Devon Park on Stanley Point. Having made such developments allowable by right in the local planning scheme, local residents had little or no say in its construction. The Council actively supported the measure, waiving reserve requirements. The matter had been approved by Council before they considered such matters as building height or sewerage disposal, and by 1967 the borough engineer was involved in negotiations to erect a sewer which would have been two or three feet off the ground to the building along the seaward side of the neighbours' sections. A public meeting was called and eventually a conventional connexion was made. The building was without the usual fire-fighting equipment and in their enthusiasm the Council had even neglected to consider this question.

Site of the proposed Devon Park development at Stanley Point, 1967. *North Shore Times Advertiser*

Devon Park in 1985. *Chris Miller*

The Council's enthusiasm for change appeared to bear little relationship to the needs of the area, and certainly no attempt was made to study and to identify any problems. There was no attempt, for example, to stimulate or even maintain industry, and the mayor of the time seems actively to have discouraged attempts to establish an industry specifically designed to help returned servicemen. On 18 May 1950 the Council received an application to build a clothing factory but being unwilling to mix industrial and residential areas they declined permission.

The area that seemed most at risk was Windsor Reserve. Council and various local authorities were continually proposing schemes for the area. The old Borough Council Chambers were demolished in 1954 and a new library and Plunket rooms built on the site. In the same year the old fountain—again designed by Edward Bartley—which had been built as a memorial to the men who died in the Boer War, was filled in and a band rotunda built in its place. It was designed by the Council Engineer A.T. Griffith, who said, "I tried to design something ornamental but with a musical atmosphere." The fence on the band-stand represents bars of music with notes showing the first bars of "God Save The Queen"!

In 1957 the Ratepayers Association suggested the building of a town hall out over the water on the edge of the reserve. In 1963 the Takapuna Lions Club proposed that a miniature railway be built there. The Council agreed before investigating its legal right to do so. There was some opposition and the matter lapsed. In March 1965 the Council commissioned a development plan for the area—it was to include a paddling pool, a sound-shell, dressing sheds, an aquarium and a seafood restaurant. The outcome was a proposal for a marineland which aroused considerable opposition. A private bill for the development was drawn up for Parliament and was opposed by Gainor Jackson who threatened to take out an injunction against the scheme. Jackson and his supporters also forced the holding of a referendum on the matter. By 1970 the developer had withdrawn his proposal. Although the marineland was not the final and biggest issue, it saw the beginning of the divisions that were to be so evident later. At this stage alliances were more fluid; for example, the Devonport Ratepayers Association was firmly opposed to development of Devonport as a high-density suburb, but supported the beginnings of Ngataringa Bay.

It is interesting to note that this belief in the power of progress was coupled with conservative politics. For example in May 1947 the Council refused to allow the local Communist party to hold open-air meetings. And in 1951 the Council offered to provide guards and patrols to protect military and naval installations during the Water-front Strike.

Apart from further schemes such as a funicular railway to the top of Mt Victoria, gondolas to North Head and a revolving restaurant on Mt Victoria, the 1960s and 1970s was a time of relatively "hard-nosed" and businesslike development dominated by the Ngataringa Bay scheme which received, until the 1970s, the support of most councillors. In the meantime the Council had time to liberalise such matters as bathing regulations, which had not been changed since the nineteenth century, when Council had passed regulations which had at one time excluded women from all beaches. During the 1920s there was no limit on the hours of bathing but swimmers had to wear neck-to-knee costumes, and people were not allowed to stand near Cheltenham Kiosk unless fully clothed.

In 1964 residents were opposed to the establishment of a tip at Ngataringa Bay but by 1968 this had become a secondary issue, as Council had approached Fletcher Holdings about a marina proposal there. In July 1969 the Auckland Harbour Board approved a plan for a $5 million development of 370 sections with water access. This signalled the beginning of organised protest on the grounds of conservation, and demands for access to information about the project. In September 1969 those pages dealing with the proposal in the Council minutes were deleted. In 1970 the Council scheme remained in abeyance although the Ngataringa Bay Empowering Bill was being nursed through Parliament. Negotiations with developers were

actively pursued by some councillors, but in 1971 two new Council members opposed to the proposal were elected, M.H. Pritchard and W.D. Titchener, and following their election and the formation of the Devonport Planning Association the old guard on the Council was gradually voted out until the former were sufficiently powerful to reverse the Council decision on the Bay scheme. The outcome of this opposition was not merely the demise of Ngataringa Bay "development" but a change of direction in the way the borough was to be managed. Those who advocated development probably did not undergo a sudden conversion to the new "doctrine", but they were sufficiently in the minority to allow people with other views of urban living to put their ideas into practice.

In many ways the demise of the schemes was a consequence of the inability to deal with opposition; there had never been such concerted opposition to a Devonport Council before, and a reluctance on the part of the supporters of development to realise that they were out of step with public opinion was revealed. An interesting result of the Ngataringa Bay controversy was the opportunity it provided for local people usually unenamoured and uncommitted to local politics to venture into the fray. Their views on the way in which the settlement might develop were less "progressive" than in the past but it is not unfair to say that as a direct consequence the amenities and unique qualities of much of Devonport have been preserved.

Ngataringa Bay development model, 1969. *North Shore Times Advertiser*

It cost threepence to travel from Devonport to Cheltenham in 1886.
The Devonport wharf in 1887. Coal is being unloaded on to carts which will take it to the gasworks. *Auckland Public Library*

Industry and Commerce

Gael Ferguson

Devonport's first businesses were farming and ship-building, but from early times it was unclear whether it would become an almost self-sufficient and independent community, or a residential suburb of Auckland. This uncertainty is reflected in a resolution of the Borough Council passed in February 1898, requiring the removal of all waterfront buildings between Stanley Bay and North Head. This was aimed mainly at the ship-builders and timber-millers, whose premises cluttered the pleasant shoreline. The resolution was not really needed, for sooner or later these eyesores withdrew voluntarily to Auckland, leaving Devonport as essentially a marine suburb, fashionable or unfashionable, but always with a character of its own.

By the late 1920s for many it was not much more than an unavoidable (and irritating) stop on the road north from Auckland, until construction of the harbour bridge in the 1950s brought it face to face with the need to define itself. Ambitious schemes for high-rise buildings and the like were proposed and usually rejected. This was a time when developments were often insensitive to the needs and wishes of local communities. The present community of Devonport has recognised itself for what it is—a residential marine suburb, earning most of its money in Auckland, with an affection for and a pride in the industries of the last hundred years, which have not wholly vanished, though they now serve rather than dominate a locality conscious of its image of continuity.

To go back to the beginning. The first economic activity in Devonport was farming—of a sort. In 1848 Devonport was placed under the Hundred of Pupuke, an administrative unit which controlled the use of waste or common land. Crown grantees, pensioners, and local Maoris of Devonport held licences to run cattle on these lands. Grantees in the 1850s included some well-known Auckland names—John Logan Campbell, Colonel Wynyard, James O'Neill—while others formed the basis of the early Devonport community—

Torpedo Bay from North Head c.1880. Brown and Sim shipbuilders can be seen on the beach. *Photo. Burton Bros. Devonport School Album*

Thomas Duder, James Hammond, I. Burgess, William Oliver and Alex Alison.

Administration of the Hundred had ceased by 1854 but cattle continued to roam freely. In 1867 the Flagstaff District Highways Board ordered that "pigs must not be allowed to remain at large on any highway, road, street or public highway within the limits of the Flagstaff District". By the 1870s the Board was administering a pound; originally located on the junction of Vauxhall Road and Church Street and run by the ubiquitous Oliver Mays (postmaster, shopkeeper, and local body politician), it was removed to Victoria Road in 1871. The cattle were largely confined to North Head by 1878, although the council was often criticised for allowing cattle on reserves. As late as the 1890s stock could be found grazing on the Triangle. In 1872 ratepayers were limited to no more than four cattle and one horse on common land, and by 1885 pigs were forbidden to roam freely.

Although land was to be an important asset after the 1870s, when increasing speculation in sub-division occurred, in the early years it was only incidental to the activities of many of the residents. The main activity was ship-building. As Thomas Walsh writes: "The coming of the shipyards to Devonport in the early sixties virtually 'made' the township, and indirectly had a big influence in making Victoria Road the centre of the business part of Devonport." The ship-builders and the ferry service have been well documented, and any discussion reads like a guide to early Devonport society. Alex Alison senior moved to Devonport in 1852 from his ship-building site in Mechanics Bay. George Beddoes opened a yard at the eastern end of Torpedo Bay in 1858. He entered into partnership with James and John Holmes who set up their own yard at the Sandspit (Windsor Reserve) in 1863. (The real importance of the latter lies with the ferry service rather than with actual ship-building.) Their brother William Holmes also started his own yard. Sims and Hoile Brown arrived in 1864 but by 1879 had opened a yard at Freemans Bay as well. Henry Niccol began in 1865; he and his son Malcolm Niccol were to play a major role in local politics. A grandson, George Niccol, continued the business well into the twentieth century, moving from below Garden Terrace to the site which was later to become the Devonport Steam Ferry Company slipway. He eventually moved to yards near the old Nelson Street wharf in Freemans Bay. Le Huquet (father and

The residence of William Holmes, shipbuilder, on King Edward Parade. This photograph is undated. *Auckland Public Library*

son); Colin Wiles; Davy Darroch, who built scows; and the famous yacht-builder, Robert Logan, all had yards—some, such as Le Huquet, until the 1920s.

Some of these ship-builders were associated with the development of a ferry service to Devonport. At first demands for a service reflected the need for access to the city. However, by the late 1860s it was clear that there was an important link between development of the "suburban" farms and the provision of an adequate service. The Holmes brothers were among the first to develop their land at the foot of Victoria road. Their speculation began a long and sometimes bitter feud betwen the inhabitants of Church Street and Victoria Road, and signals the beginning of a fierce price-cutting war between companies.

Mr John Reed provided the first service, an open boat capable of carrying twenty people, which sailed to and from the Sandspit area on Fridays. Perhaps the fact that they might at any time be called on to row the boat left the passengers dissatisfied, for they soon

petitioned the Provincial Council for action. During the 1850s the Council advertised for tenders but only one was offered, in 1860 by a Captain Kreft. He ran the paddle steamer *Emu* which unfortunately sank in the same year on an expedition to Motutapu. Again the Council petitioned. Mr Carr of Official Bay built the *Phoenix*, but his service was declined and the local inhabitants were forced to make do with private boats.

In 1864 the Holmes brothers went into action and in doing so initiated the steady eclipse of the original Church Street settlement. They built a hotel (the Flagstaff) and wharf at the foot of Victoria Road and ran a cutter from there to the city. Their real interests were revealed when they subsequently advertised the sale of sections at "Devonport village", at the same time issuing a prospectus for the "Waitemata Steam Ferry Company" and undertaking to build a steam ferry, the *Waitemata*. In retaliation George Beddoes and Thomas Duder, among others from Church Street, formed a company promoting use of their wharf. They opposed a government subsidy of the service, and through control of the local licensing committee refused to grant a licence for the Flagstaff Hotel unless the brothers guaranteed a twice-weekly service to Church Street. Within seven months the Holmes's company was in disarray. The visitors to the hotel did not eventuate, and they were forced to turn to haulage work. John Holmes, who disagreed with the move away from passenger transport, constructed a new boat, *Enterprise I*, and launched a new rival company in December 1864. There followed a price war which eventually meant the sale of the Waitemata Company to John Holmes. Triumphant, he persuaded the Provincial Council to pay for a wharf at the site of the present wharf, and refused to run a service to Devonport East.

The eastern wharf was difficult to navigate at low tide but, undaunted, the inhabitants launched a counter-attack. A Mr Cobley began a service from there in 1869 but it failed and was taken over by the Holmes brothers within two months. The "East" tried again, forming the "Auckland and North Shore Ferry Company" with the

Victoria Wharf — is the ferry loading or unloading? c.1909. *Miss G. Williams*

steamer *Jane*. F.J. Somerfield, a shareholder, commissioned the first composite ship in New Zealand, the *Devonport*, but again the company failed and was sold to the Holmes brothers. However, a second Auckland and North Shore Steam Ferry Company was floated in 1872 and by 1876 had bought out the Holmes brothers. The new company was not well managed and in 1881 a number of residents, including E.W. Alison, set up the Devonport Steam Ferry Company. The company ran a large fleet, including the *Tainui, Arawa, Takapuna,*

Devonport and later the *Kestrel*. Its monopoly was to be challenged only once, by George Quick who commissioned the *Eagle* and the *Osprey*, and began the construction of the Bear Gardens near Garden Terrace as an extra attraction. After an eight-month "war" Quick sold out to E.W. Alison.

The company continued supreme, extending into vehicular ferries after 1911, with vessels such as the *Goshawk*. The vehicular wharf was constructed in 1927 (before that time pontoons had to be used)

This photograph of the steam ferry graveyard at Brown's Island is undated. Here lie the skeletons of *Victoria, Takapuna, Birkenhead, Tainui* and *Alexandra. Devonport School Album*

and Devonport's importance as a transit point for goods and traffic was assured for the next thirty years. After the construction of the harbour bridge the company was sold to North Shore Ferries and many of the ferries were scrapped or retired. Only the *Kestrel* and the *Baroona* of the original fleet remain in service.

On land, horse-drawn trams were introduced in the 1880s. The first section of wooden tracks to Cheltenham were laid in 1886 but the company was never successful and was taken over by the Duder brothers in 1887. In 1894 the tracks were removed and sold. Paul Hansen, the representative of the British Traction Company, who had been involved in the provision of electric trams for Auckland City, received a monopoly from the Borough Council for the introduction of electric trams. Hansen achieved nothing and in 1908 the option was transferred to the Devonport Transport Company.

Parson's horse-drawn bus carried passengers from the Devonport wharf to Cheltenham and Narrow Neck, c.1901. This photograph was taken from where the Esplanade Hotel now stands and features H. Anderson (first driver) and Andy Parsons (second driver). *Devonport School Album*

It too failed, and for a brief moment the Council toyed with the idea of providing a service. However, other problems such as paying for an adequate water supply were enough to persuade them to leave it to private enterprise.

Road transport was more successful, and for many years there were several large stables, most of them near Victoria Road. The tram company had stables in William Street. Blacksmiths and the stables run by Parsons could be found in Clarence Street. In the 1880s a coaching service to the north was run by the Patterson brothers. The Duder brothers, who owned a shop on the corner of King Edward Parade and Church Street, also ran a cartage business, principally for coal and heavier goods. E.W. Alison had introduced buses by the end of World War 1, but because the Takapuna Borough Council wished to protect the tram service which ran from Belmont to Bayswater the buses were not licensed to run to Takapuna. Alison retaliated by introducing a fleet of Hudson cars. In the 1920s the Glassey brothers were running the Bluebell Bus Service; the Orewa-Waiwera White Star Service operated from Anne Street, and the Marine Suburbs Transport Company delivered such things as firewood.

Special dispersal auction of teams and equipment in Victoria Road by Mr W. Parsons, c.1899. *Devonport School Album*

The "up-to-the-minute car" advertised by Patterson's Motor Garage, c.1920. *Devonport Public Library*

The Bluebell bus service, King Edward Parade. The buses ran from Victoria wharf to Narrow Neck and Victoria Park. *Paul Titchener collection*

The Kauri Timber Co. yard opposite Anne St. in 1900. Parson's carrying service poses outside. *Devonport School Album*

W. Brown, Devonport carrier, 1924. *Paul Titchener Collection*

Another major "industry" was the brickworks at Ngataringa Bay. There had been earlier works, for example in Brick Bay (Stanley Bay), but the Duders' works were by far the largest. The Duder brothers owned grazing land (undeveloped until the 1930s and 1940s) which later became the Victoria Park subdivision. In about 1875 they were approached by a brickmaker to whom they awarded a five-year lease. He proceeded to make bricks on a small scale in wooden moulds which were dried and then burned in clamps. He eventually left for the Thames goldfields and the two brothers took over the business. The works became fully mechanised with scows calling at a wharf below the site of the present naval housing. It produced bricks, sewer and drainage pipes (the brothers often contracted to the Council for drainage and road works), and ornamental pottery made mainly by two men, Tom Cooper and I. Savidan. In the 1930s the works were taken over by the Crumm brothers who operated a large works at

New Lynn. They leased the Duders' business for several years but produced nothing, their main aim being to control competition from the North Shore. A relatively minor clay and brickworks was also run by the Gas Company on the opposite side of the Ngataringa Bay.

Manufacturing was not confined to private individuals. The Devonport Borough Council made a brief and ill-starred foray into the supply of electricity. While the fears of one critic who felt that "by its Bolshevism or public ownership (the Council) is destroying man itself ..." were apparently unrealised, the Council's involvement was poorly timed and badly managed. In 1914 the Electricity Supply Corporation had been given the option to supply electricity in the borough. The building and generator was located on Church Street and was supplied with the necessary coal by the Duder brothers. The generator proved to be a noisy affair, and the company encountered considerable protest when it tried to raise charges. The Council

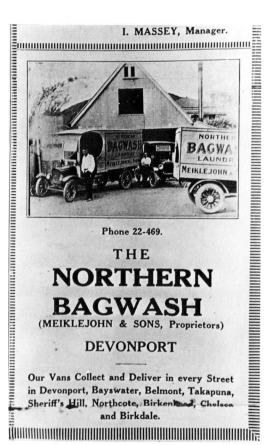

An advertisement for the Northern Bagwash,
c.1928. *Devonport Borough Council*

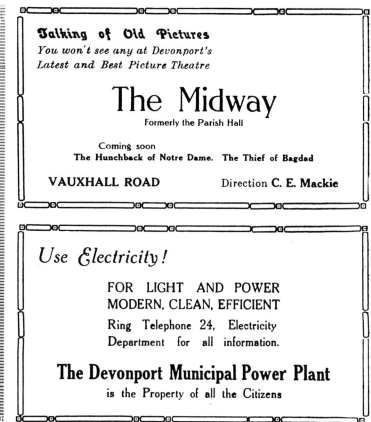

A couple of classics are advertised at the Midway.

An advertisement for Shelma ice cream. The
factory was located on the site of the present
dairy in Victoria Road. *Devonport Museum*

stepped in and bought it in 1922, but they too experienced difficulties almost immediately, for it was at that time that the whole question of metropolitan supply authorities was being debated. After 1926 the plant was used only as an emergency supply and in 1929 the machinery was sold. Meiklejohn and Sons acquired the building for their "Northern Bagwash Company", which by 1949 had been renamed the Northern Laundry Company.

Another well-known concern was the Takapuna Dairy Company located on Victoria Road. Owned by the Massey family (initially in partnership with a Mr Hamer), the company was established about 1902. As the borough grew the local supply of milk was replaced by supplies from Tamaki and Hobsonville. When the Government took over the pasteurisation process the Dairy Company modernised their equipment and began the Eldora icecream factory. Branches were formed at Dargaville and Whangarei, but about 1960 the business was sold to General Foods.

Concentration on these industries tends to overshadow the small businesses and shops that operated in Devonport from about the

1870s. Originally local families were provided with produce on an informal basis. Alex Alison senior, for example, grew produce which he gave or sold to local people. Later there were to be Chinese gardens on the hill next to the old State Theatre and also overlooking the golf course near Lake Road. In the 1880s it was also possible to identify a number of local shopkeepers—Mrs MacGuiness the dressmaker; Alex Geath, tobacconist; James Holmes, greengrocer; Coombridge Robinson, bootseller; John Jarvis, grocer; H. Lennard, greengrocer; L. Spinley, stationer; and Jack Cogan, blacksmith. Apart from the Flagstaff and Masonic hotels (founded in the Devonport "war"), there was also the British Hotel, opened in 1873 and located near the present post office. Oliver Mays, who had run a shop from his various homes in the borough, was also responsible for the post office until it was placed in a permanent building on the site of the present Council offices. James Sibbin set up a publishing and printing office in 1896 and the *Waitemata Times* began printing in Devonport in 1901.

Fifty years later Percy's soft drink factory could be found near the present Sterling Stores, a favourite meeting place for children having their lemonade bottles filled. Johnson and Noble were well-known grocers on the corner of Victoria Road and Clarence Street. There were Ford's tearooms which catered for the weekend visitors; Johnson's bakery; Bogues who ran a mail service to Silverdale and who still had stables in Fleet Street; and Howard's fish store. Cogan the blacksmith still continued, as did Bond's timber yard. The various bakers—Buchanan, Craig's, MacGregor's and Lanes—not to mention Crabb's stable in Bond Street, the Devonport Mutual Stores, William

A group of laden Devonport posties pose on 1909. *Anne Sutton*

These blacksmiths look the part in front of their Clarence St shop. *Paul Titchener collection*

Scott's Family and Shipping Butchers, Oborn's OK Shoestore, the Red Post Furnishing Company, R.N. Melville, auctioneer, and W. Cox's "Kia Ora" fruit store, should all bring back memories for many people.

Shops developed in other areas of the borough beside Victoria Road and Church Street. However, competition from outside and the advent of supermarkets, as well as the changing character of the settlement, have meant the closure of a number of these shops. Others have been taken over by more esoteric businesses. The result is a situation little different from what it was fifty years ago. The appearance of the shops is almost identical, even if the functions of many have changed. Such new ventures as co-operatives and "The Works" consciously preserve and even draw upon this continuity.

The little shop on the right was once the Devonport post office. *Richardson Album, Auckland Institute and Museum*

Buchanan's bread delivery, c.1930. *Keiser family*

E. Ford's refreshment rooms on King Edward Parade. *Richardson Album, Auckland Institute and Museum*

Victoria Road, c.1920. *Auckland Institute and Museum*

The older industries relied on the ability and desire of the community to change their environment in order to prosper. The brickmaking industry modified the area around Ngataringa Bay while more obvious changes are associated with the navy and their workshops. The shipbuilders probably had the least impact.

While local industries altered or died out, the willingness to alter the environment did not, and this has been discussed in an earlier chapter. Here it is worth noting that in recent years, "economic activity" is very much more sensitive to the needs and structure of the community. However, while there is an emphasis on the past this has not precluded Devonport from developing new activities. While for most residents financial reality exists in the exigencies of a job in the city, their undoubted pleasure in the settlement is based, in part, on the fact that Devonport is not, like many places in Auckland, a mere dormitory suburb. Devonport has managed to retain or foster the vitality that went with its "industrial" past and which was lost during the 1950s and 1960s.

Malcolm's cash store on Lake Road at the top of the intersection of Old Lake Road. Date unknown. *Paul Titchener collection*

Three scenes from the Mt Victoria Signal station.
1. George Taylor, signalman from 1905-1923. *Paul Titchener collection*
2. In the thirties. *New Zealand Herald*
3. In the fifties. *New Zealand Herald*

The Garrison

David Barratt

It was 1840, after Governor Hobson had raised the flag at Point Britomart on 18 September and thus founded the city of Auckland, that a signal mast was erected and a powder magazine built on the northern side of the Waitemata Harbour, convenient to the deep water anchorage favoured by the naval ships. The boat landing, called Sandspit, was near today's Ferry Wharf. The area was called Flagstaff.

On 13 September 1841 Lieutenant Robert Snow of the Governor's staff moved ashore with his wife and family to take charge of the growing facilities, and he was appointed signalman. Soon Able Seaman Thomas Duder joined Snow at Sandspit and became his assistant. This was the start of a garrison which grew and developed and changed side by side with the original settlement. Flagstaff became the Borough of Devonport and in conjunction with the civilian settlers of Devonport and their descendants has produced a society where the civil and military continue to mix and work side by side in harmony.

In 1886, when Devonport became a borough, there was considerable military activity in the community. Since the 1860s, when colonial forces were raised on the withdrawal of imperial troops, there had been a succession of militia and volunteer units, with very few regulars to advise them, on the shores of the Waitemata. These included Armed Constabulary, Auckland Volunteer Coastguard, Auckland Artillery Volunteers, Auckland Naval Artillery Volunteers and Devonport Naval Artillery Volunteers. A pair of field guns had been positioned on North Head and Robert Snow's original installation had grown into the Naval Reserve (now Windsor Reserve), complete with caretaker's house, blacksmith's workshop, two-storey barracks and carpenter's shop with a capstan for hauling up small vessels, a purpose-built boatshed and launching ramp for the brand new torpedo boat—and, of course, a flagstaff. A jetty and torpedo storage facilities had also been built at Torpedo Bay.

A naval presence was definitely in evidence.

An illustration of Calliope Dock which appeared in *The Illustrated London News* on 21 April 1888. *The Illustrated London News*

The Auckland Harbour Board had started to construct their dry-dock below the cliff at Calliope Point. The dock was formally opened on 16 February 1888 and Admiral Fairfax, Commander-in-Chief of the Australasian Station, said:

It will give me great pleasure to report to the Admiralty the completion of this great work—the largest dock in the Southern Hemisphere and the use it will be to Her Majesty's Ships, especially in time of war, when they can be docked, securely protected by your forts and torpedo defences. I trust that it may be the means of drawing to your fine harbour men-of-war and ocean steamers of all nationalities, and thus add to the wealth and prosperity of the beautiful Town of Auckland. (Long and prolonged cheers)

Above: Spar torpedo boat. 1884. *Naval Museum*

But surely the most dramatic activity on the garrison scene of 1886 was the construction of defences for Auckland Harbour which was progressing apace and in common with similar defences at major ports in New Zealand and other parts of the Empire. It was during the latest "Russian scare" of 1885 that the plans produced by Major H. Cautley RE were adopted and work started on building fortifications and gun batteries at Fort Bastion and Fort Resolution on the south side of the harbour and at Mt Victoria, Fort Takapuna and North Head in Devonport Borough. The largest project was to be the controlling position and three batteries on North Head.

We may be thankful that the threat of invasion came to nothing. However, in Devonport the fortifications remained, some being modernised and adapted over the years to meet the needs of defence during the 1914-18 and 1939-45 wars. Muzzle-loading guns were replaced by breech-loaders. Guns with a slow rate of fire (called "disappearing" guns because they were lowered into their gunpits for reloading and then raised again to the firing position), were reinforced by more modern weapons. A whole variety from ships' cannons and field guns through 8-inch, 7-inch, 6-inch, 4-inch and assorted smaller quick-firing guns with searchlights, minefield control and anti-aircraft

New Zealand Permanent Artillery relax in their barrack room at Torpedo Yard, 1899. *W.L. Ruffell*

Upper right: A thirteen-ton disappearing gun being unloaded for installation on Mt Victoria in 1899. *Auckland Public Library*

Lower right: District gunners, North Head, 1899. *W.L. Ruffell collection*

guns have all been installed at times in the forts at Devonport during the years when an army garrison was in residence.

In times of tension and in wartime the batteries were fully manned but in calmer times the garrison would be reduced for care and maintenance of the peacetime installations. In 1902, for instance, the permanent militia comprised the Submarine Mining Establishment consisting of twenty-five NCOs and sappers and Permanent Artillery of fifty NCOs and gunners under Captain McKenzie. These men were stationed at Fort Cautley (North Head) and Fort Takapuna (Narrow Neck).

Above: This naval shed was built about 1863, and burnt down in 1897. *RNZN*
Below: The new Naval Reserve with the caretaker's house to the left and the Auckland Harbour Board workshops and dry dock behind. June 1901. *RNZN*

During the two World Wars the Narrow Neck Military Camp, which had grown up beside the old Fort Takapuna, became the depot for large numbers of soldiers who were on their way overseas. After 1945 the army presence in Devonport was reduced again progressively during the next thirty-five years. Many of the defence guns were removed or sold for scrap. The final artillery unit at North Head was the 9th Coast Regiment, Royal New Zealand Artillery, which disbanded in 1958 and ended some seventy-three years of gunner occupation, leaving the Navy in possession of the summit. Meanwhile the name Fort Cautley had been transferred from the summit battery area of North Head to Narrow Neck Camp.

There too, things were changing, for in August 1963 the Navy's wartime training establishment HMNZS *Tamaki* was moved from Motuihe Island in the Hauraki Gulf to occupy some of the surplus facilities at Narrow Neck. In April 1979 the Army "marched out" from Fort Cautley to their new headquarters in Takapuna and today have relatively small accommodation needs at Narrow Neck in what is now the Navy's principal training establishment.

On the naval scene there had been a move by the Devonport Borough Council, back in 1890, to acquire the land which then formed the Naval Reserve. Auckland at that time was competing with Sydney for the right to become the naval base for the Australasian Squadron and so considerable pressure was brought to bear on the Devonport Borough Council to waive their claims to the land. In the end, the Mayor of Devonport offered four acres of reclaimed land in the vicinity of the new dock at Calliope Point as an alternative site and this offer was accepted by the Admiralty. That reclaimed land was to form the basis of the future naval base. The only immediate action was the removal of the caretaker's cottage from the old Naval Reserve to the new one and no further development occurred for many years. However, the old naval barracks and carpenter's shop burned down on 11 April 1897 and thereafter the old Reserve was transferred to the Borough and became the Windsor Reserve in 1911.

Stanley Bay and the Naval Base, c.1930. In the rear can be seen Ngataringa Bay reclamation for the naval storeyard. *Lackland photo*

HMS *Philomel. A.W. Skinner*

HMS *Achilles* alongside at the Devonport dockyard, 1937. *RNZN*

The Harbour Board gradually improved workshops and facilities near their dock, while the Admiralty built a store nearby and encouraged the Harbour Board by paying an annual subsidy which would ensure priority use of the dock and workshops for naval ships. The deep water jetty was built in 1908 and then the huge 80-ton sheer-legs, which could be seen from everywhere and which were used so little, were raised. Progress was slow and despite the new Naval Reserve being declared a "Naval Base" in 1909 it is remarkable that only four times during the First World War were Calliope Dock and the workshops actually used for HM ships.

From 1921 onwards the pace changed with the formation of the New Zealand Division of the Royal Navy and the arrival of the Dominion's four-funnel cruiser HMS *Chatham* based at Devonport. The old cruiser HMS *Philomel* arrived at Devonport the same year and became a permanent feature as the alongside training and depot ship. The Naval Base was at last a reality. The coal-burning *Chatham* was replaced by two oil-burning D class cruisers and they in turn were replaced by the two *Leander* class cruisers which were to distinguish themselves in World War Two. Calliope Dock was lengthened; workshops, stores and repair facilities were improved;

World War II activity in the enlarged HMNZS Dockyard. *RNZN*

The harbour boom and anti-submarine nets extending from North Head to Bastion Point during World War II. *Naval Museum*

the mighty sheer-legs, after being used twenty-five times in twenty-six years, were lowered with a spectacular splash in 1934; and in 1936 the whole property, except for the dry-dock itself, was transferred from the Harbour Board to the Admiralty. HM Dockyard, Devonport, had arrived.

The outbreak of World War Two brought activity to the defence areas in Devonport such as had not been seen since the "Russian scare" days of the 1880s. After Pearl Harbour and the fall of Hong Kong and Singapore, during the build-up of the American forces in the South Pacific, the physical defences of the approaches to Auckland were strengthened and the naval base facilities increased so that repairs of New Zealand and allied naval ships could be undertaken. When peace came to the Pacific again, the Devonport Naval Base was up-to-date and well equipped to provide all the needs of a small modern navy. Permanent barracks and the Naval Hospital had been built, as had a complete stores depot on reclaimed land. The navy's fuel oil storage had been hidden away within the cliffs and a tunnel had joined the dockyard to the stores depot. The dockyard itself had been enlarged and equipped for its wartime level of work and even the Harbour board's dry-dock had been lengthened once more so that

American cruisers could be docked.

Since 1944 the major noticeable changes have been the scrapping of the old cruiser *Philomel*, which had been in service afloat since Queen Victoria was on the throne; the further reclamation of land in Ngataringa Bay for the creation of a sports complex, and the construction of a new wharf to complement the fragile Calliope Wharf in 1908. In the peacetime era of over forty years ships have come and gone—some brand-new, some second-hand, and even one rented. The day of the prestigious cruiser has disappeared and the all-purpose frigate has taken the place of the larger ship. The people look much the same as their predecessors forty years ago; the men and women of the navy and their civilian associates in the dockyard and stores depot who together make up the garrison of today, are just one or perhaps two generations removed from the garrison of World War Two and only four generations away from those who manned the torpedo boat, drilled at the old Naval Reserve or stood by the gun batteries in the garrison duties of the "Russian scare". But if Lieutenant Robert Snow were to land by boat at Sandspit this year, he would be very confused indeed.

Left: A naval officer on his way to work. *Chris Miller*

Right: The naval base in 1985. Note the extensions on the far right to Calliope wharf. *RNZN*

Nº 885. Teachers & Pupils, Devonport School.

The first Devonport primary school in Kerr St, c.1935. *Devonport School Album*

74 *THE SCHOOLS AND CHURCHES*

The Schools and Churches

Lois Westwood

Why tie the churches and education together? One explanation is that at the beginning of European settlement early Devonport had neither church nor education. Parents taught their children what they could, and God-fearing families held their own private devotions. Church and school began together and grew up together in Devonport, with beginnings too intertwined to separate.

The North Shore had no schools at all until 1849, when St Mary's Catholic College opened at Shoal Bay. But Devonport boys hoping that the long distance, the lack of roads and the need for every pair of hands to break in the land would save them from a formal education had reckoned without the pioneering spirit of their Victorian parents.

The early Anglican settlers may have had no church, but they certainly had their worship. The drawing room of Alex Alison resounded with the voices of Bishop Selwyn and Bishop Patterson, who were rowed across the harbour to tend their flock.

Then in May 1854 fifteen Anglican families decided to found a church and school for the district, and in less than a year a small building with weatherboards and battens was erected at the junction of Church Street and Vauxhall Road. Bishop Selwyn agreed to appoint a minister and schoolmaster and the Rev. E.H. Heywood began duties on 18 May 1856. He must have been a man of boundless energy, for his parish extended to Albany and the Wade river! Each Sunday after morning service he would walk to Stokes Point, Northcote, and then to Lake Takapuna to conduct services there. His school was named St Mary's and became known to the locals as Flagstaff school. The Anglicans ran it for a year before receiving Government financial aid on the condition that children of any denomination could attend at a fee of one shilling a week.

By the time the Anglicans had built their first church there were enough Methodist settlers in Devonport to warrant ministers on circuit from Pitt Street being rowed across to conduct services in private homes.

Holy Trinity Church and parsonage, 1888. *Richardson Album, Auckland Institute and Museum*

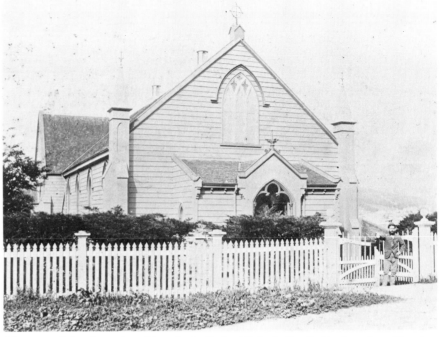

The second Presbyterian Church, built in 1890. *St Paul's Presbyterian Church*

By 1859 the difficulty of staffing schools in Auckland had become so great that the Education Board adopted a policy of giving eighty acres of land free to every qualified teacher entering its employ. Devonport was lucky to have the stable influence of the Rev. Heywood, who taught for six years before being succeeded by Oliver Mays, who stayed for three. In 1861 St Mary's had a roll of nineteen and an average attendance of nine. Only boys were taught at this time; it was considered that girls did not require a formal education.

At this point the Methodists began to hold their services in the Anglican schoolroom and on 4 January 1865 held a meeting where it was decided to raise funds to build a chapel on the side of Mt Victoria. On 13 August 1865 the new Methodist chapel was opened by the Rev. T. Buddle. The following month the Anglicans conse-crated a larger church which seated 180 people.

It was now the Presbyterians' turn to become established in Devonport. Other denominations had first built a church before attracting a minister, but the Presbyterians appointed their minister first. He was the Rev. John Wallace, who began his duties in March 1866. An advertisement was placed in the *Southern Cross* stating that "Divine Service for settlers of the Presbyterian faith will be conducted in the public schoolroom until such time as a church can be erected". The hard-working Rev. Wallace and his parishioners used the schoolroom for no more than a few months. A building contract was let to Mr Hiram Pitts in December 1866 to erect a church on the corner of Church and Cracroft Streets. It had to be enlarged only six years later.

In 1867 gold was discovered at Thames, which resulted in a lean time for Devonport, as many local residents left to try their luck at mining. For some reason the Methodist population was particularly affected. The remaining congregation was unable to support the church and it was closed down.

Two years later the education authorities invited the Flagstaff Highway Board (the forerunner of the Devonport Borough Council) to consider establishing a "Common School for Boys" in Devonport. The Methodist chapel had passed into the hands of the mortgagee and was bought for £200 to become the school building. The first headmaster, Mr Pierce Phillips, was appointed at a salary of £150.

Devonport School (amalgamating with St Mary's) opened on 17 January 1870. The fees for arithmetic, geography, history, reading and writing came to twenty-one shillings a term. Within three years the school employed three teachers, two of them women, so it was not surprising that by January 1874 the school committee decided to apply for a £50 grant to build a girls' school for the district. The chapel building required additions in 1875, 1876 and 1878 to meet the increasing roll. In 1878 the Government abolished the collection of fees from parents. Free education had begun.

Meanwhile the Methodist Church, kept alive by a small group who held cottage meetings led by visiting ministers from Auckland, managed to buy land in Beach Road (later named King Edward Parade) and opened another church in March 1877.

Devonport's population continued to grow. By 1881 the Catholic congregation, which had been holding services in private homes for the past twenty-six years, began to hold their services in the school. The present Anglican Church of the Holy Trinity was consecrated on 11 March of the same year. The new Methodist church was also getting tight at the seams, and the roll at Devonport School reached 302.

The Salvation Army's earliest Devonport records note a meeting held in the Assembly Hall in Beach Road in 1883. The meeting was "disrupted by hoodlums"—but the Army was here to stay.

Opening of the Salvation Army Hall in Hastings Parade, 1909. *Paul Titchener collection*

In 1885 the Methodists bought a site in Church Street and moved their building there, where they added a transept and installed the Rev. Spence, who became the first resident minister responsible not only for Devonport, but also for Northcote, Birkenhead and Takapuna.

Now another denomination made an appearance. Members of the Congregational Church (who used to travel across the harbour to the main church in Beresford Street) met in Captain Fielder's house in Victoria Road and decided to build a place of worship which could also be used as a school. This they did, although the depressed financial times combined with big debts nearly swamped them. But after the arrival of the Rev. Richard Laishley, a remarkable man, the parish was revitalised and grew and flourished under his care. He was a vigorous seventy-three when he arrived, and he worked there until his death nine years later.

By 1889 the Presbyterians who were prospering under the influence of the Rev. A. McCallum, who had presided over their flock for the past six years, moved their building back on to the original site and built a larger church there.

The next major expansion was made by the Catholics. Although Devonport had a large Catholic population from the many Irish settlers who were employed in military service or at the Beach Road shipyards, they were the last of the major faiths to build locally, as the main parish centre was at Shoal Bay. In February 1893 a meeting was held in the school to discuss a church for Devonport. An ideal building was available—the little Church of St Francis de Sales, built by Bishop Pompallier in 1866 and sited at the Symonds Street cemetery. It was loaded on to horse-drawn wagons, carted to the Auckland waterfront, and floated across the harbour on a punt. It was then transported to the present site alongside the Presbyterian Church in Albert Road.

Here we have the only recorded disagreement betwen churches in the borough and it must have been a "Ngataringa Bay" of an issue at the time! The land had been granted to the Presbyterian Church

A church group outside St Leo's convent, c.1906. *Anne Sutton*

by the Crown, but as the Church had not used the land and was now well established in Church Street, the Catholics had applied for part of the title. An argument developed which was not resolved until the Minister of Internal Affairs ruled that part of the land could be used by the Catholics. So the Church of St Francis de Sales was brought there.

Up till that time religious instruction for Catholic children had been given by two Sisters from St Mary's in Ponsonby. Every Sunday they travelled across the harbour by rowing boat—later ferry—until 1896, when they bought a cottage and section opposite the church. The cottage became a convent and one room was used as a school. Late in 1897 it was decided to build a school—the present St Leo's Hall—which was opened in April 1898. The school was divided into two sections: St Leo's Academy and the Parish School. Pupils attending the academy paid fees but children attending the parish school did not. A curtain divided the classrooms separating academy

The staff at Devonport School, 1889. *Auckland Public Library*

pupils from parish children, but they shared the same teacher—an arrangement which continued for seventeen years.

In 1899 the Salvation Army bought a building in Hastings Parade, which remains their base to this day.

In 1904 Devonport School opened an infant block and the roll rose to 736. The overcrowding was by now so serious that the early situation was reversed—now every church hall in the borough was turned into a classroom.

By 1909 Devonport School was the second largest in New Zealand, and Stanley Bay School was opened as a side school under Devonport School's control. The first head teacher, who also doubled as infant mistress, was twenty-year-old Miss M. Barr, who coped with ninety-eight pupils with the help of one pupil teacher.

In 1910 another school opened. This was Cheltenham College, a private school for young ladies (there were a number of very wealthy residents in Devonport by this time), offering day and boarding

THE SCHOOLS AND CHURCHES 79

"Castlereagh", Cheltenham College for Girls, is the two-storey building near the centre of the photograph. The street is Vauxhall Rd. *J.B. Miller*
Inset: "Castlereagh" in 1972, shortly before its demolition. *New Zealand Herald*

facilities. It opened in the stately house "Castlereagh" in Vauxhall Road and closed, partly because of the influenza epidemic, in 1919.

In 1910 the Presbyterians built a Sunday School in Stanley Bay and ceased administering Takapuna when St George's Parish Church was opened there. Stanley Bay School became independent of Devonport School and the following year its building was extended.

By the start of World War One Devonport School had 877 pupils. The next year St Leo's was registered with the Education Department and the curtain was finally drawn on the academy side of the building. From then on St Leo's became a wholly parish school.

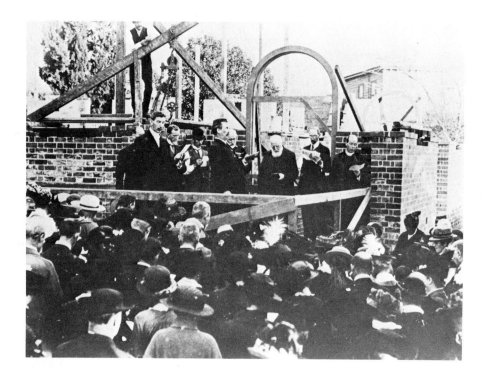

Left: The laying of the foundation stone of St Paul's Presbyterian Church on 29 July 1916. *St Paul's Presbyterian Church*

Right: Vauxhall School pupils and teacher outside their army shed — their temporary accommodation before completion of the school building in 1920. *Paul Titchener collection*

In 1916–the year of the fiftieth jubilee of their church in Devonport–the Presbyterians decided to build a bigger church in Albert Road. The building was completed in 1917. Two years later a new Catholic Church which could hold 500 people was consecrated on the site alongside, the early wrangle between them long forgotten.

By the end of the war the Devonport School roll reached 911 and the following year Vauxhall School was opened. Robert Carnachan, the first headmaster, actually held classes for his 196 pupils in an artillery shed at Narrow Neck army camp while the school was being built. The new building, designed for 200 pupils (fifty per class) was too small even before it opened–with a roll of 300 children. But the School Committee raised £500 from a Queen Carnival which with the addition of a Government subsidy provided funds to lay out school grounds which equalled the finest in the country, with tennis courts, basketball courts, rockeries and playing fields.

Another private school opened the same year. Cheltenham Collegiate, occupying a large house by Holy Trinity Church, offered facilities for twelve boarders and thirty-four day girls ranging from five to the early teens, and for boys up to the age of seven. It closed three years later when the board was unable to obtain a suitable replacement for the headmistress when she moved to Australia.

In 1924 Holy Trinity divided itself, forming the parishes of St Michael at Belmont and St Augustine's at Stanley Bay. Next year Vauxhall School doubled its classroom space by building a new wing.

Moving on to the 1940s, members of the Four Square Gospel Church began to hold their meetings in the Buffalo Hall, finally building their own church in Albert Road in 1952. At the end of the 1960s they changed their name to the Christian Revival Crusade—an independent church with links to similar churches throughout the country.

Sadly, the Congregational Church declined. The attractive building was sold and parishioners were forced to travel out of Devonport for their worship.

Until the arrival of the private car and television the churches in Devonport provided major focal points of social life in the community. They still do—but up to the fifties there were more time-consuming activities in which parishioners could join—drama productions, sports teams, vocal groups, or craft circles. One local lady remembers putting her name down at the age of fifteen to join the waiting list for the Holy Trinity Church choir.

The Methodist Church acknowledged community changes in the 1960s when it decided to sell the land in Church Street and Stanley Bay and Vauxhall Rd and build a modern church and meeting centre on the corner of Lake Road and Owens Road. Opened in April 1971, the multi-purpose areas which form part of the complex are used all week for all manner of community activities.

The most recent church to open its doors in Devonport has been the Jehovah's Witnesses, who bought the State Theatre for their Assembly Hall in 1978.

During the past decade all the schools have added new buildings. Devonport School was completely rebuilt in 1970, but Stanley Bay preferred to keep its historic old buildings and modernise inside, adding two new blocks to the original school.

The inter-church co-operation which has been a feature of the borough during the past century is still as strong as ever, with a number of shared services during the year and shared carol services at Christmas.

The links with education are still maintained. The major churches in Devonport provide a Bible in Schools Programme with ministers and trained lay people holding a half-hour class in local schools one morning each week.

Father Furlong at Rangitoto, c.1933. *Anne Sutton*

Art

Cheryll Sotheran

The story of art in Devonport resembles a microcosm of national developments in art through the 150-odd years of this nation's European history.

From early settlement times—when the distinctive silhouette of the Devonport promontory provided the colonist artist, working in the European watercolour tradition, with the variety of texture and mass essential for an effective panorama—to our own period, when the encouragement of contemporary artists through festival exhibitions and competitions involved the suburb in the modernist debate, this apparently sleepy suburb, set apart from the busy city centre by an expanse of water, was almost always included in early views of Auckland Harbour painted from various vantage points on the "mainland". The majestic and terrifying landmarks of the Sublime—mountains, lakes, waterfalls, natural wonders such as could be found in the thermal regions—were not available here: even the threatening presence of recent volcanic activity advertised by the multiple cones

of the region, with Rangitoto looming as the most notable and most ominous, did not appear to create a sense of unease in the colonial recorder: the emphasis was on serenity and calm, an effect easily communicated by rendering the sheltered waters of the Waitemata, the faintly exotic but comfortable symmetrical outline of Rangitoto—and of course the elegant silhouette of Devonport itself.

Devonport first appeared as the acknowledgment of the importance of the place in the practical business of settlement. The slender flagstaff from which the suburb took its early name can be seen in such early representations as Edward Ashworth's watercolour of the arrival of the two immigrant ships *Duchess of Argyle* and *Jane Gifford* in 1843. Here the viewer looks from the obligatory high point, marked on the left by a touch of the exotic in the presence of a group of "natives", across the embryonic town, past the spire of St Pauls to the completely barren and unpeopled slopes of the Devonport peninsula. The artist has evened out the land mass and emphasised the crater on the summit of Mt Victoria, setting to one side a slender white mast. In contrast to the cleared brown scrubby slopes and neat white buildings of the settlement on the near shore, Flagstaff/Devonport retains a sense of mystery—the unexplored, the green, bushy-covered 'other' the colonists saw as their ever-present challenge. The slender mast sounded that challenge, made the European mark.

As settlement progressed, the North Shore became the place for mildly alarming expeditions—a safe taste of more dangerous expeditions taking place throughout the rest of the country. From the barely tamed land across the water of the earliest representations, the suburb became in artists' eyes more clearly a guardian, or look-out.

In *The Lively Capital*, her book on early Auckland, Una Platts commented on John Kinder's wash drawing of a group of very civilised early settlers on the verandah of Mr Keven's country house, set on the slopes above the town:

> The gentleman shown on the verandah, looking through the spyglass, has been probably sharing the preoccupation of most Aucklanders—wondering whether the signal of Flagstaff Hill across the harbour, gave the good news of a ship coming in and bringing letters from Home …

Two water colours by the colonial artist Alfred Sharpe gave a clear indication of the development of the settlement at Flagstaff. In the late 1850s Sharpe paints a serene panorama of the Waitemata, with Devonport occupying the bulk of the middle ground. The larger outline of Mt Victoria, with the ill-fated Mt Cambria at its side, and the smooth rounded headland of North Head remain free of any signs of settlement, apart from the flagstaff itself, and the cleared bush with sporadic outbreaks of scrub and isolated trees. But our cover painting, by the same artist, 'View from Auckland Domain 1877', which looks from a high viewpoint over diminutive houses to the harbour, with Flagstaff and Rangitoto beyond, shows quite extensive foreshore development, with several large dwellings on higher ground.

J. Hoyte's view of Auckland in 1873 reveals the same pattern of settlement. It affirms the sense of serenity and beauty which early Aucklanders derived from, or perhaps imposed on, their harbour: William Swainson in *Auckland and the City Adjacent* commented: "the harbour is by no means devoid of natural beauty. Commonly there is an excess of wind, but not infrequently … a perfect calm for a time prevails … This seen, the Waitemata presents a landscape of placid beauty which it would tax the imagination to surpass."

The suburb of Flagstaff, retaining as it did that sense of a place for adventure, a place to go on expeditions, gradually lost its slightly alien quality, and became a place not visited but lived in, not painted from across an expanse of water, but the inspiration for numerous artists to make pleasing views of places within the suburbs. The Devonport wharf, Cheltenham and Narrow Neck beaches and, further afield, Takapuna, gave ample opportunity for the expression of the unthreatening picturesqueness of late colonial painting. In this, the art reflected what early residents felt about the quality of life which could be experienced in what was now fast becoming a sleepy seaside suburb.

> In the eighties we lived a homely life and quietness prevailed. Nobody seemed to be in a hurry. The only people who rushed were those who considered they were late for the ferry. Sometimes the ferryman pulled in the gangway, unloosed the ropes and started on time, leaving the crowd walking down the wharf … This was a punitive measure.
>
> (E.W. Alison: *A New Zealander Looks Back*)

In terms of art nothing happened for much of the early part of the new century to change this sense of tranquillity, unless the opportunities offered for quiet reflection and the pursuit of learning in such a secure and undisturbed environment could be seen (with justification) as providing fertile ground for the growth of new ideas, as well as the opportunity to perfect practice.

Harry Cobley's house. A water colour by John Hoyte, painted in 1870. *Alexander Turnbull Library*

Rex Fairburn visiting Christchurch in 1947. Denis Glover is waiting inside the car. *Pegasus Press, Alexander Turnbull Library*

Perhaps this is why Devonport, and the North Shore as a whole, became, as the century approached its mid-point, something of an intellectual centre—a source, and sometimes a refuge—for adventurous minds. In the field of art A.R.D. Fairburn, who has the dubious distinction of being if not New Zealand's first, then undoubtedly one of New Zealand's most outspoken art critics, formulated his forthright views on the relationship of New Zealand art to the growth of modernism on the international stage in the tranquil setting of Devonport's foreshore. While Fairburn will probably be best remembered by posterity for his notorious dismissal of Colin McCahon's religious paintings of the 1940s as "graffiti on walls of some celestial lavatory" (*Landfall* Vol. 2 1948), he made a considerable contribution to the infant stages of art writing and teaching in this country, as well as making his own contribution as a practitioner. His column in the *Listener* during the 1940s produced such confident declarations as "Art has its own laws, but it can't be disassociated completely from life". (*Listener* 1946)

> I doubt if it is possible for any man who hasn't played Rugby football to get the fullest enjoyment out of watching a good game, and I doubt if any person who hasn't at some stage tried to draw, or to smear pigments on a surface, or to model in clay can really understand and appreciate the lovely texture of a painting by John Piper ... in brief, it is unhealthy for any complete gulf to exist between the artist and the common man, however widely they may be separated in point of skill and sophistication ... I should like to see the arts being practised in much the same way as we practise football ... (*Listener* 1946)

Fairburn's approach combined a blend of wilful philistinism with an insistence on technical correctness, which contained more than a hint of resistance to creeping modernism. While not exactly reactionary, his affirmations of the normal and the need to remain in touch with the common man as he defined him; his use of forthright, unsophisticated language and terminology, and his suspicion of such modernist tendencies as were by then being demonstrated by the art of such painters as McCahon, fitted well with the growing interests of the art community of Devonport.

Practical achievement was given much emphasis, and it was from the firmly established background of a dedicated group of local art practitioners—amateurs in status, but not in determination—that in the 1950s the Devonport Festival Society was created. These festivals were marked from their earliest years with an adventurousness in terms of media: Maori crafts, for instance, were acknowledged for what must have been one of the first times as having a value and importance which has only now been universally acknowledged in the 1980s. The Devonport Festival Society made a clear statement in 1965 of their importance, and offered a prize in that area: "A New Zealand-wide competition among Maori weavers to make traditional Maori kits from entirely traditional materials using traditional designs."

In such important but uncontroversial ways, the Society brought into Devonport much influential art—national figures such as Peter Smith, Jan Nigro, Ralph Hotere, Keith Patterson and Barry Brickell came to display work or to judge competitions. I remember from my youth the displays of paintings hung in Windsor Reserve: a taste even to my uneducated eye of a cosmopolitan and sophisticated world beyond the childhood Devonport experience of endless sun, swims and enormous icecreams from the Shelma milkbar.

But apart from worries about where the money was to come from (a worry apparently effectively put to rest by the enlightened Devonport Borough Council, who began to give financial support from 1959) the winds of controversy did not blow on this sunny scene until the Festival, now operated on a North Shore-wide basis, and with private sector as well as local body sponsorship, found in 1973 that the decision of the judges for that year's art award—Hamish Keith, Michael Dunn and Richard Teller Hirsch—did not meet with the approval of the major sponsor, a local contractor and self-confessed "philistine", James Davern. The award went to a work by David Armitage, a painter of modern and uncompromising tendencies, with

The Devonport Festival Society held the annual Arts Festival on Windsor Reserve in 1969. *North Shore Times Advertiser*

an ability for effective colour juxtaposition and sharp social comment not usual in Devonport/North Shore Festival entries. Mr Davern, at an unforgettable award ceremony in the Holy Trinity Church Hall, rendered artist and audience speechless by proclaiming his dislike of

the award-winning work. Later in the local press he avowed that it wasn't the work so much as the fact that it didn't fit his idea of the theme for the competition:

> I was not offended by the painting, but what I had envisaged for the award was a painting showing driftwood, or Great Barrier Island, or perhaps an environmental theme ... all it shows is two women lying on the beach. I can't see where the sea comes into it.

But the damage was done: Devonport had witnessed, in microcosm the emergence of several major issues of modernist art: the debate was given even more point by Davern's almost symbolic purchase, not of Armitage's winning work, but of the technically competent, but unchallenging marine subject of the second place-getter, David Barker.

After this brief flowering of controversy, and the demise of the Festival itself in 1975, art in Devonport settled down. The Ngataringa Bay campaign saw the production of original posters by two leading artists, Don Binney and Patrick Hanly, and the running of a large and successful art auction as part of the fund-raising festival in 1982.

Local people continue to paint, sculpt, and exhibit for their peers, and for the local community, and these days several rising figures in the New Zealand art scene live and work in Devonport, deriving no doubt the same blend of proximity to the sophistication and stimulation of the major centre just across the water, and the tranquillity and chance for reflection that was evident to our colonial forebears.

Don Binney's splendid Ngataringa Bay poster. *Don Binney*

Andy Barrett at work on her porcelain ware at The Works, 1985. *Chris Miller*

Members of the North Shore Cricket Club playing on the old pitch at Cheltenham flat in 1893. *Paul Titchener Collection*

Sport

Paul Titchener

Devonport could well claim to be the "cradle of sport" in New Zealand—a presumptuous claim perhaps, but the contribution to the sporting history of the country made by this little isthmus is out of all proportion to its size or population. Here is the oldest cricket club, the oldest soccer club and the oldest rugby league club in New Zealand; the rugby club is the oldest in Auckland, and the third oldest in New Zealand; the golf club is the second oldest in Auckland; the rowing club (now relocated on the shores of Lake Pupuke) is the oldest in Auckland; the yacht club and the men's bowling club each are the third oldest in Auckland; and an ill-fated baseball club (the first and probably the only such club in New Zealand) was founded in 1889. The Takapuna Jockey Club was formed in 1881, at that time only the second in Auckland, and at its meeting held in May 1911 legal on-course bookmakers operated for the last time. It ceased operating in 1934.

Why was Devonport so prominent? The answer can be tracked back to 1845 when the 58th Regiment of Foot, commanded by Colonel (later General) Robert H. Wynyard, whose descendants were to play an important part in the sporting development of the borough, arrived in Devonport. The soldiers of the 58th Regiment were mostly Irish, and brought to Devonport the Irishman's competitive spirit and love of ball games. This interest soon led to competition between the soldiers and the sailors from warships which spent long periods anchored in the harbour. The sailors soon challenged the soldiers to games of football, which were encouraged by their officers, as they gave the men physical exercise, and allowed the officers to gamble on the results. The field on which these hard-fought, often brutal games were played was a grassed area just to the east of the old Devonport wharf, where Flagstaff Terrace is now. The game they played was based on the age-old *kick-baa*, a curious mixture of kicking and running with the ball whose origin is lost in the mists of time.

The Devonport ground was only 100 metres long, but great were the games played. The young men of Devonport watched with avid interest and were soon competing with the servicemen. After the outbreak of the Waikato land wars the military presence in Devonport was greatly reduced, and the old football ground became no longer available because of the establishment of the Royal Navy in the area. Undeterred, the locals found a suitable field near Duder brothers' Store in Church Street where the parking area for the Masonic Hotel is now sited. There they continued to play football, and in the summer cricket, which they had also learnt from the soldiers. It was not long before clubs were formed and the history of organised sport in Devonport began.

CRICKET

The first club to be formed was the North Shore Cricket Club in 1864, a year before the Mauku Cricket Club at Patumahoe. Both clubs were established by military and civil officers who had brought their love of the game with them from England. In early New Zealand cricket tended to be introduced and fostered by the official classes — the public servants of the colonial governments and later by the officers of the various army regiments and, to a lesser extent, the Royal Navy. These men had been educated at schools where cricket was compulsory. The first cricket game played in New Zealand was at Petone in 1839, the players all being public servants. But it appears that the game did not develop there, as no clubs were formed or further games recorded.

The first club captain of the North Shore Cricket Club was Captain G. Wynyard (son of Colonel R.H. Wynyard) of the 68th Regiment, who was responsible for securing a pitch between Albert Road and the Waitemata Golf Club. The fortunes of the club fluctuated according to the availability of military personnel, but the first recorded game against another club was in 1867, when a city club called Blackstones, made up of lawyers and law clerks, beat North Shore. A return game was played at the Auckland Domain, the North Shore players travelling across the harbour in rowing boats to St George's Bay on the Parnell foreshore, and then walking to the domain. Just after the game started, heavy rain fell and the match was called off. A very wet and dejected North Shore team walked back to the harbour to row home.

It was not until 1870 that another inter-club game was played, as the owner of the land where the club's pitch was laid wanted it for hay. Forced to move, the club laid a new pitch on the Cheltenham Flat, a popular sporting area just to the east of where Tainui Road is now, behind the sandhills which then skirted Cheltenham Beach. Here matches were played every Saturday throughout the summer. The pitch was watered from a well dug about 500 metres away, local boys being employed at the rate of a penny per bucket to carry the water.

Through the 1880s the land around the pitch was being sold for private housing and the club went into a period of comparative inactivity. In 1890, the newly formed Borough Council agreed that a pitch would be laid on the Devonport Domain ground if the club would pay £50 toward the cost. A total of £6-18-0 was raised by the club, and the Council laid not one, but two pitches which are still used to this day. This was the turning point in the history of the North Shore Cricket Club. A pavilion was built and the Club became a major force in Auckland and New Zealand cricket. Players such as Ces Dacre, Verdun Scott, Jack Cowie, Martin Snedden, Roy Harford, Don Coleman, Ross Morrison, Cam Maingay, and Alan Richards all won Auckland representative honours, and the first four became famous names in New Zealand cricket.

RUGBY

The type of man attracted to cricket is also attracted to the other great English game of rugby. Those young men who played football on the paddock in Church Street included W.L. Lees, who was so active in the Cricket Club. He, together with R.H. Nolan (later Sir Robert Nolan), was instrumental in forming the North Shore Rugby Club in 1873. The date may have been earlier — some reports state

Right: The Devonport cricket pavilion, c. 1905. *Alexander Turnbull Library*

The Devonport rugby grounds, c.1900. *Alexander Turnbull Library*

the North Shore Club "secured a touchdown, which Mr Rees failed to turn into a goal", to quote the newspaper report. This was the end of the game and the North Shore Rugby Club, in its inaugural season, remained unbeaten. But the years were not easy for the Devonport club. Its playing strength was dependent on the availability of soldiers and sailors stationed in the area—a fact relevant to the present day. But the club continued to play teams from across the harbour with mixed results, and in 1883 was one of the co-founders of the Auckland Rugby Union, along with Grafton, Ponsonby, a reorganised Auckland club, and, surprisingly, Tauranga.

The financial depression in the 1890s had a big impact. Jobs in the local shipbuilding yards were lost and many young men moved to the Thames goldfields and to the South Island. But the men from the services kept the club going throughout this period, and in 1899 it had recovered enough good players to win the Auckland Rugby Championship, the only time in its long history. Now that the club plays in the North Harbour Union, this will remain its sole championship under the auspices of the Auckland Union.

In 1903 the old dressing shed was replaced by a training shed on the south-eastern corner of the domain, and in 1905 this in turn was replaced by a more commodious building on a section bought by the club betwen the Domain and Beaconfield Street. However, during a lean period, a concerted attempt was made in 1909 by the newly-formed Rugby League Club, Albion, to take over both grounds and training shed. The rugby club officials and players strenuously resisted this move, which resulted in a brawl between the two codes on the Domain in August 1909. The Council called a meeting the following Wednesday night in the Council Chambers, where again punches were exchanged. The Council compromised, giving each code an adjoining ground on the Domain, resulting in an often uneasy relationship which lasted until the early 1960s, when the league club moved to Bayswater.

In its 133-year history, the North Shore Rugby Club has had five players selected to play for New Zealand—J.P. Gerrard, D. McKay,

1870, others 1872—but certainly in 1873 the North Shore Rugby Club was reported in the leading newspaper of the day as being formed to play 12-aside rugby football. On 26 July 1873 the first true game of rugby, albeit with 12-aside teams, was held between the North Shore and Auckland clubs at Cheltenham Flat. The result was a 0-0 draw. The return game, with 15 players a side, was held on 16 August 1873, on a ground in the long-demolished Albert Barracks. The redoubtable W.L. Lees kicked a goal and the Auckland team walked off the field leaving the North Shore Club victorious. A third match was arranged at Devonport on 30 August, and after two hours play,

P. Cunningham, B. Johnstone, and W. Shelford, with many others representing Auckland in various grades. Although the club now plays in the recently-formed North Harbour Union, the contribution made by the North Shore Club to the development of rugby in Auckland (and New Zealand) will never be forgotten.

SOCCER

The start of association football in Devonport was directly the result of a rugby injury. The player concerned was the fine sportsman, Charles Craven Dacre, who was born in Sydney in 1848 and came to New Zealand in 1859 with his father, an officer in the Royal Navy. Dacre was sent to England to complete his education and excelled there in both cricket and football. He returned to New Zealand in 1870 and became a skilled player of the North Shore Rugby Club, being selected to play for Auckland in 1876. His association with rugby ended suddenly two seasons later when he broke his leg while playing against Grafton on the old Cheltenham Flat ground. A witness and fellow player, Dick Duder, said that "the crack of the breaking leg sounded like a pistol shot" in the cold winter air. Dacre was carried home on a door ripped from a neighbouring barn. He never played rugby again, but turned to soccer. In May 1886, together with Messrs W.R. Goudie and F.J. Whittaker, he called a meeting at the old Flagstaff Hotel to form an Association Football Club. The meeting was successful and a team was selected. The new club was called the North Shore Association Football Club, but to avoid confusion with the rugby team, it played under the name "Devonport". A pitch was laid out in the old bear gardens in Queen's Parade and practice games began. The first serious game against another club took place on 11 June 1887 when the North Shore Club played against a recently-formed club from Grafton, called Carlton, at a ground in Remuera. The result of this historic game was Carlton 6-Devonport nil.

The North Shore Association Football club flourished through the 1890s, mainly because eleven players were easier to find than fifteen for rugby, and many older rugby players turned to soccer. The pitch at Queen's Parade was too small and in 1897, a ground was made available on the Devonport Domain. With the new century the club continued playing in the Auckland Football Association championships, its senior team bolstered by naval ratings stationed at nearby HMS *Philomel*. At Belmont, a junior club was formed and many games were played between the two clubs over the year. On 12 April 1933, the two amalgamated under the name "North Shore United Association Football Club".

The years of the Second World War were difficult but with the return of peace the North Shore Club quickly re-established itself, and has since played a dominant role in New Zealand soccer. A significant development for the club was the decision to acquire its own ground at the former site of the Gas Company's brickworks at Ngataringa Bay. In 1982, Dacre Park (named after Charles and his son Ces Dacre, a double New Zealand representative in soccer and cricket) was opened and New Zealand's oldest soccer club had entered a new, exciting phase in its history.

RUGBY LEAGUE

Rugby League has also enjoyed a prominent position in Devonport's sporting history. In 1909 the first league club in New Zealand, the Albion, was formed in the borough. The founders were men who had long been associated with rugby and as stated above, relationships between the two codes were far from cordial. Over the years the club has competed with mixed success in the Auckland competition and several of its players have represented New Zealand. Perhaps its greatest achievement was in 1939, when seven members of the Albion Club went overseas with the Kiwi team to tour England.

BOWLING

The Devonport Bowling Club was founded in 1895, the third oldest in Auckland, and since that time has occupied part of the Devonport

Bowling at Devonport, c.1890. *Alexander Turnbull Library*

PLAYERS FOR CLUB TROPHIES —
— WAITEMATA LADIES GOLF CLUB.
29/6/33.

Success for the Waitemata Ladies Golf Club in 1933. *Paul Titchener Collection*

Domain. In early years the greens were also used for croquet by the wives and daughters of the members. The North Shore Women's Bowling Club which was established in 1947, constructed greens adjacent to the Waitemata Golf Club house. This is the oldest women's bowling club on the North Shore.

GOLF

The Waitemata Golf Club was established on 21 August 1905. It was the second club in Auckland and the first on the North Shore. After early problems over finding sufficient space for an 18-hole course, the club leased the former race course at Alison Park from the Council in 1934, after the Takapuna Jockey Club had been wound up. After installing floodgates and pumping equipment during the 1960s to drain the former mudflats, a 5306-metre 18-hole course was developed with a men's par of 70 and a women's par of 72. The Waitemata Ladies' Golf Club was founded in 1910 and shares the course with the men.

YACHTING

Yachting has always been popular in Devonport. The first yacht club was the North Shore Sailing Club, founded in September 1894. In 1901 the name was changed to the North Shore Yacht Club, but dissension developed between Devonport and Auckland members, with the result that in 1905 Devonport members of the club formed the Devonport Yacht Club. In 1921 the North Shore Yacht Club transferred its activities across the harbour and changed its name to the Akarana Yacht Club, now the Royal Akarana Yacht Club, one of Auckland's senior clubs. The Devonport Yacht Club flourished until World War I, but then became dormant until 1923. In 1926 it acquired its hauling-out area on the foreshore, a repair yard used by the Steam Ferry Company. The club has since thrived and today is one of the most active in New Zealand, organising many off-shore and coastal races for keelers.

ROWING

The North Shore Rowing Club was founded in 1874, the oldest in Auckland and one of the pioneer New Zealand clubs. The first clubhouse was erected where the Windsor Reserve is now, and the first boat owned by the club was a four-oared gunwale gig. This boat was not fast, but proved ideal for training young rowers. The first competitive boat was a four-oared outrigger skiff bought from the Thames Rowing Club, and in this the club enjoyed many successes. In 1892 the clubhouse on Windsor Reserve was moved to a site west of the Devonport wharf, but during a high tide backed by a strong westerly the shed was flooded as well as being badly damaged by a scow. It was removed and rebuilt on the site near Duders Beach, where it remains, now used by the Calliope Sea Scouts. The fortunes of the club fluctuated with the interest of local young men in rowing but a major decision in the 1960s to move to the more sheltered fresh water of Lake Pupuke ensured a new lease of life, and today the North Shore Rowing Club is one of the premier rowing clubs in New Zealand.

Above: The *Janet* off Torpedo Bay in 1904. In the background is Mr Watson's house, which was later destroyed by fire. *Henry Winkelmann*
Below: Watching in comfort. Stanley Point residents watch a race in progress on the Waitemata Harbour, 1953. *Alexander Turnbull Library*

The grand opening of the North Shore rowing season in 1900. *Vaile photo. Auckland Institute and Museum*

The Vauxhall Tennis Club, with the Takapuna racecourse in the background. *Paul Titchener Collection*

SWIMMING

Swimming has also been a popular sport in the borough. The first swimming club, the North Shore Amateur Swimming Club, was founded in 1897. The first secretary was that prominent sportsman in rugby, soccer and cricket, C. Dacre. Other clubs were founded only to disappear. The North Shore Club continued to promote competitions, mainly at the tepid pool in the city but it also organised beach swims, its annual race along the Cheltenham Beach becoming a popular event.

TENNIS

Tennis has always been well patronised. The Devonport Tennis Club was formed in 1880 on a drained part of the Domain, near Vauxhall Road. At the height of its popularity in the 1930s the club operated six grass courts cared for by two groundsmen. A comfortable pavilion was built, but the cost of maintaining the courts, with competition from two hard courts at Vauxhall and Ngataringa, proved too much for the old club and in October 1963 it was wound up. This was a sad end for one of Auckland's pioneer lawn tennis clubs, but tennis clubs at Stanley Bay and Vauxhall today cater for playing needs.

HOCKEY

Men's hockey has been played at Stanley Bay for over forty years. The history of the local game dates back to 1924, when the Stanley Bay Primary School took it up. A pitch was laid on reclaimed land at Ngataringa Bay, now called Stanley Bay Park. Hockey proved so popular with the boys that even after leaving school they continued to play and the Stanley Bay Hockey Club was formed. The Navy also formed its own club. Former players such as Syd Mainland took up coaching and the Stanley Navy Hockey Club became a major force in Auckland hockey. Many club players represented Auckland in the various grades and one, half-back Jim Palmer, went on to play for New Zealand. Today the Stanley Navy Hockey Club has been absorbed into the North Shore Hockey Club, whose headquarters are now at Takapuna, but Stanley Bay Park is still used by women hockey players in winter and cricketers in summer.

Motor cycle racing on the Takapuna racecourse in 1927. *Paul Titchener Collection.* **Right:** Fred Johnson, Clerk of the Course, Takapuna Racecourse, *Barry Coleman, Devonport Borough Council*

MOTORCYCLE RACING

The sport which made Devonport a household word during the heady years of the 1920s, when the world relaxed and tried to forget the horrors and personal losses of World War I, was motorcycle racing. It may have been noisy, dirty and smelly, but it attracted huge crowds to the borough, even by today's standards, enriching the Ferry Company and local businesses. The first grass-track motorcycle meeting was held on 26 January 1920 on the course owned by the Takapuna Jockey Club and was promoted by the Auckland Provincial Motorcycle Club. The programme, of six races, was watched by over 8,000 people. This was the first grass track motorcycle event held in Auckland and proved highly successful. The next meeting was attended by nearly 20,000 people and for the next eight years Devonport became the Mecca for motorcycle enthusiasts, and gained an international reputation. Many famous international riders competed, and major European and American motorcycle manufacturers entered machines. At the 1929 meeting Percy Coleman set the

world grass-track one mile record of 44.35 seconds on an 8-valve Harley Davidson—a record which was to stand for forty years.

HORSE RACING

Horse races were also held on this course from 1881 until 1934, when they ceased following the death of a jockey. Greyhound meetings were also moderately successful there, while professional foot races attracted some public interest. But none of these captured the excitement and crowds as motorcycling did.

Devonport's unique position in the history of New Zealand sport remains unchallenged by any other local body. The sports-minded residents of the borough and the administrators who encouraged them by providing facilities must not be forgotten, and a tangible reminder of their foresight is the fact that today the Borough of Devonport has the highest ratio of recreational sports grounds to total land area of any local body in New Zealand.

Thomas Howarth's house on Cheltenham Beach, built in 1908. *Henry Winkelmann. Auckland Institute and Museum*

Architecture

Jeremy Salmond

Devonport is a borough with undeniable character and a special quality that sets it apart from the rest of metropolitan Auckland. All the same, it would be an exaggeration to claim that its streets are lined with architectural gems from the past 100 years. Some of the town's character derives from its insular and waterside location, but perhaps its special virtue is a pleasing mellow ordinariness in its buildings, enhanced here and there by architectural delights.

Early growth in the borough took place on the original farm allotments surveyed within the Parish of Takapuna, around competing areas of commercial activity in Church Street and Victoria Road and the land in between. As growth spread north from the harbour edge, the original farms were subdivided and sold for housing. The layout of Devonport streets reflects this pattern of development and the street names recall those who played a part in the town's growth.

Construction of houses is a good indicator of the national economy, and Devonport's houses reflect colonial booms and recessions. The earliest period of marked growth was the 1870s when timber was a major export trade. Then followed the recession of the 1880s, with slow growth through the 1890s and a marked increase in house-building during the first fifteen years of the twentieth century. By 1916 the waterfront was fully built up, as was most of the land each side of Calliope Road and on the slopes of Mt Victoria and North Head. Remaining large tracts of land in North Devonport were developed in the period between the wars, and since 1940 house-building has been sporadic, taking place on difficult sites, replacing houses lost by fire or decay, and in the last few years by subdivision of original sections to allow new houses to be built in former backyards.

A particular feature of the last decade has been the move toward renovation of older houses, which has been accompanied by a steady and dramatic rise in property values in Devonport.

Until 1940, commercial growth generally followed the pattern of house-building, reflecting confidence in the borough and supplying local services in each neighbourhood. Since then, however, new commercial buildings have been rare and of no great distinction, and many of the small local shops—dairies, butchers, and the like—have disappeared.

The former Duder house at 11 Church St. A fine family home of the 1860s. *Chris Miller*

So we look to our past for architectural pleasures. Few of the earliest houses remain, but enough to show that simplicity of form and detail were both a virtue and a practical necessity. The former Duder house at 11 Church Street is a fine large family house of the 1860s, with steep gable roofs, now thoughtfully preserved. Good examples of workmen's cottages of the 1870s are 13 Buchanan Street and 4 Kerr Street ("Slope Cottage"). They illustrate the simple hipped roof over two main rooms with two or more rooms behind under a lean-to or gable roof. "Superior" cottages of the same vintage are exemplified in 28 Church Street where a steep pyramid roof covers four rooms.

The 1880s saw the development of the villa style house in which main rooms were separated by a passage from front to back—a plan which lasted well into the second decade of the present century. A typical house of the 1880s is 16 Eton Avenue. The most common type of villa was, however, the "bay villa", in which a room projected forward on one or both sides with a large bay window on the end

Top left: 13 Buchanan St. *Chris Miller*
Top right: Slope Cottage, 4 Kerr St. *Chris Miller*
Bottom left: 16 Eton Avenue. *Chris Miller*
Bottom right: 28 Church St. *Chris Miller*

Top left: 9 Ewen Alison Avenue. *Chris Miller*
Top right: 1 Kapai Rd. *Chris Miller*
Bottom left: 6 Garden Terrace. *J. Salmond*
Bottom right: 10 Patuone Avenue. *Chris Miller*

Left: 26 Cheltenham Rd. *Chris Miller*
Upper right: 28 Albert Rd. *J. Salmond*
Bottom right: Plan for Mr F.A. Wharfe's house in Calliope Rd.

wall; this window eventually became part of the wall itself. Devonport has some excellent houses of this type illustrating many of the possible alternative designs.

No. 9 Ewen Alison Avenue (ca. 1882) is an early bay villa and it is interesting to compare this with others in the borough to show how the type evolved over a period of some thirty years. No. 1 Kapai Road (ca. 1900) shows how the main roof first covered the bay window, while 6 Garden Terrace and 10 Patuone Avenue are fully evolved bay villas: elegant houses with modest decoration.

No. 28 Albert Road is a "double bay" villa of 1900 with generous proportions, and 41 Stanley Point Road shows the ornate turreted style with bay rooms on two sides (the "corner-bay" villa). One of the finest late villas in the borough is 26 Cheltenham Road with carefully fretworked brackets in gables, under sunhoods and on the verandah.

FRONT ELEVATION

House styles changed dramatically after the 1914-18 war. The popular taste was for the North American bungalow at first, or for houses in the English "arts and crafts" style. By the 1930s rather more exotic influences prevailed—"Spanish mission" and "moderne"—alongside more restrained bungalows.

Devonport bungalows are generally rather conservative, and not altogether typical of the exuberance which was found elsewhere, but a good example is 54 Old Lake Road. Some of the better bungalows were architect-designed, for example 48 Clarence Street (by J.M. Walker) and 48 Calliope Road (by Edward Bartley). The "arts and crafts" houses were also products of an architect's style; 6A King Edward Parade by W.A. Cumming is one of exceptional quality.

Many architects have contributed to the Devonport environment, the best known perhaps being Edward Bartley, who designed not only many houses but also the very fine Presbyterian Church in Albert Road. Others included Fred Souster in the early twentieth century; H.L. Bates whose finest house is undoubtedly 18 Huia Street; Daniel B. Patterson; Sholto Smith and T. Coulthard Mullions; Cecil Trevithick, R.W. Kibblewhite, R.A. Abbot, M.K. Draffin and H. Rhodes Robinson.

6a King Edward Parade. *Chris Miller*

15b Second Avenue. *Chris Miller*

8 Albert Rd. *Chris Miller*

Devonport also has a considerable number of houses designed by the well-known Group Architects, including the notable Rotherham House at 27A Rutland Road and 29A Glen Road by Tim Peterson. A more recent style is 15B Second Avenue by Jack Manning.

In the late nineteenth century most houses were built from stock plans supplied by the timber companies, or taken from plan books; their builders were local men, operating in a small speculative way. Among those who made their mark on Devonport were Jas. Logan of the well-known boat-building family; E.J. Dowdy, A.L. Burrett, P.R. Grahame, Mulholland, J. McKay, and E.S. Gittos. Grahame built the handsome corner bay villas in the street that bears his name.

Not a few buildings in the borough have been moved from other sites, one at least having come from the Coromandel (8 Albert Road). 19 St Aubyn Street has had at least two previous locations, and the Church hall behind St Augustine's in Calliope Road stood originally in Church Street.

Larger buildings in the borough have at best a comfortable familiarity, and many can be identified in early photographs. The former telephone exchange in Clarence Street is well-proportioned and an excellent candidate for conversion to commercial or professional use.

In recent years the borough has operated creative town-planning policies, which have been administered with great care to encourage conservation of existing buildings and to ensure that development fits the scale and texture of the town.

The "scale and texture" of Devonport's houses. A 1985 view from Mt Victoria. *Chris Miller*

A wood engraving of women voters outside the Devonport Borough Council in 1893. *Canterbury Museum*

Women of the Borough

Sarah Campion

Early New Zealand women are "almost invisible" in the history books, but we can learn something of their lives from family tales. Jocelyn Young recalls the anecdote of her grandmother, Mary Jane Mays, being confronted by a Maori one night when her husband Oliver was out on patrol. "A big mokoed Chief came in and she sat petrified. After a long silence, the old man came forward and laid his mere on the table beside her. He smiled and nodded: then she smiled."

Later, in one of Devonport's first wooden houses, the intrepid Mary Jane bore nine children, and raised all but one. She died in her late eighties, having taken a cold bath as usual that morning. Like all settler women, she milked, made her own butter and bread, scrubbed and cleaned, sewed and knitted, as well as helping to create in Auckland's "first marine suburb" a replica of the Victorian society she had left behind at Home.

Ewen Alison's mother took him to public functions as "part of his education"—an education she began briskly one morning by saying:

"Ewen, you are five years old today, so you walk up to Devonport School and tell Colonel Smith the headmaster that you are a new boy."

Discipline at this newly-found school was sternly Victorian, as Isabel M. Cluett recalled years later: "The entire school assembled to witness the unfortunate writing victim receiving his punishment, sprawled across a desk with the master's hand on his collar." Women teachers brought in a gentler influence, and soon outnumbered the men. Three will be long and lovingly remembered: Miss Jane Grant, BA ("Scaly"); Mrs Wildman "in her floor-length black frock" conducting the prize-winning school choir, and Mrs Barnes at Vauxhall, who annually decorated every blackboard with a Christmas theme.

Private girls' schools throve in the new settlement, run by impeccable Victorian ladies: Miss Rush, Mrs Franklyn, Miss Mathews—"girls had to wear gloves on the street"; and Mrs Dean, who founded Cheltenham College. Freda Shaw, who was born at "Ingleside" when her grandfather owned it, and later went to school there when it was renamed "Castlereagh", remembers the spacious beauty of the house.

The hockey team from Miss Mathew's School, Jubilee Avenue. The girls, alas, were anonymous, as is the date on which the photograph was taken. *Devonport Museum*

This fine house at 16 Church St became Cheltenham Collegiate School for Young Ladies from 1920-1923. It was demolished in the 1930s. *Miss G. Williams*

Another pupil recalls that it was soon dubbed "Cats' College" by irreverent locals. Many Devonport girls finished their schooling in town, at St Cuthberts or Auckland Girls' Grammar; and Pat Wynyard, now in her seventies, still recalls the thrill of transferring to the new school Takapuna Grammar, when it opened in 1926 — "boys and girls were kept separate in the playground".

Devonport's founding fathers — Alison, Mays, Burgess, Buchanan, Macky, Brown — lost no time in building churches and Sunday schools, according to reports; but the busy women behind the scene do not

A game in progress, with Miss Mathew's team in white. *Devonport Museum*

Alex Alison jnr. and his family. *Dr A. Armitage*

Dame Sister Mary Leo, famed tutor of opera singers, is a granddaughter of Malcolm Niccol. She was a pupil at St Leo's Convent. *Joyce Keely*

often appear, though there is a memento of one Martha Buchanan in a water colour depicting Devonport School in its early days. Mr Cavell remembers that his two grandmothers, Mrs Myers and Mrs Bishop, came over from Parnell to start the Salvation Army, which still remains on the site given by Mrs Sinton in 1902. Sisters of Mercy also came over the water, from St Mary's Convent in Ponsonby, and began Catholic education in a cottage on Mt Victoria. They taught school subjects by day and gave music lessons at night. Three early teachers were Sister Mary Peter Burns and Sister Mary Columba Prendergast, both from Ireland, and Sister Mary Stanislaus Carmody from Queensland. A later, lovingly remembered Superior of St Leo's Convent was Mother Mary Josephine Kenny—"a great educator, gifted and artistic". She executed some murals in the parish church that have now been painted over; but St Mary's still cherishes one of her water colours, a view from the Convent to the slopes opposite, that was done the evening before she died in 1938.

Women's political education began to flower in 1893 when, after a long, bitter struggle, New Zealand was the first country in the world to grant them a vote. A contemporary wood engraving shows some of them outside the old Council Chambers having just exercised this right. "I was so flustered I put the mark against the wrong name!", one lady is reported as saying to a newspaper man: but the confusion may well have been more in his mind than in hers.

MEMORIES

Old residents recall Devonport as a village—"everyone knew everyone else". Grazing cows abounded. Mrs Edwards remembers her brother collecting theirs from Mt Victoria when school ended and "stopping to play on the way home". Most women had fowls, vegetable plots, and orchards. Mrs McGregor tells of some bad boys raiding Mrs Cassey's fruit trees, where she had hung nine newly-made Christmas puddings.

Domestic life was becoming easier. Water was now laid on; the bath water no longer smelt of fish: and children were no longer sent to beg drinking water from "Old lady Bryce's well". Grannies and aunties claimed that tap water "tasted"—but drank their tea all the same. Gas also was laid on and mothers took becolded children to the gasworks, making them inhale tar to clear their throats. "Going to town" no longer meant crossing in a whaleboat to buy a month's stores, but a short trip by ferry. "Boys sat at one end, and girls at the other—there was not much mixing but loads of fun", according to Mrs Johnson, and fog sometimes kept the passengers "just drifting around the harbour singing songs". There was little work for local girls except going into service, or helping Mrs Ford in the Irresistible Tearooms. Many worked in town. Coming back late was no problem in those placid days; Mrs Jackson remembers walking down Queen Street from the City Library: "My father brought the brake to the ferry and drove me home."

Village fairs with merry-go-rounds and maypoles were held on what is now the Domain. Beaches were the rendezvous in spring and

Looking south across the harbour towards Mt Eden, with Calliope Rd in the foreground, Wynyard St (*left of centre*) and Clarence St in the middle distance, 1886. *Auckland Public Library*

A photograph from the *New Zealand Graphic* of 4 March 1905, showing a group of maypole dancers at the Devonport Village fair. *Auckland Public Library*

A sweet stall at a church fete held at the Takapuna racecourse c.1901. *Vaile photo. Paul Titchener collection*

E. Ford's Irresistible Tearooms, King Edward Parade, in 1920. *Mrs Stella Dixon*

"Dockers" celebrating at the Calliope dock. *Richardson collection. Auckland Institute and Museum*

A picnic on Windsor Reserve, c.1919. Mrs Scott and the young Verdun Scott can be seen *(centre right). Mrs A. Scott*

CHELTENHAM BEACH
DEVONPORT AUCKLAND No 1845.

Above: Holiday time on Cheltenham Beach. *Price Collection, Alexander Turnbull Library*
Right: Ola and Elsie Clark on Cheltenham Beach, 1914. *J. Bassett loan, Alexander Turnbull Library*
Opposite: A fine day on Devonport Beach in 1935. *Auckland Star*

summer—"on Guy Fawkes night everyone came to Cheltenham". Men and children swam; but, as swimming women were frowned upon, they just paddled and dipped "dressed from neck to knee with little skirts attached", according to Mrs Jellie. One local eccentric thought hot-air baths better than sea water, so put his wife in one. "It was not to her liking, she was a bit of a character herself."

Dance at Victoria Hall, October 1918. Perhaps to welcome the Armistice? *Mrs A. Scott*

Victoria Rd residence of Mr Edward Bartley, c.1884. *Richardson album. Auckland Institute and Museum*

Other characters remembered were Mrs Lee, who used her sunshade in church and an old lady in black who kept urging Mrs Henderson's mother not to give children new bread: "It will line your stomach like a ball of putty". Mrs Henry Swan was considered a bit odd for refusing to share her husband's yacht up a Henderson creek, preferring a more civilised life in Carisbrook Flats. Henrietta Evans remembers a character of a different kind, her girl-hood friend Mrs Cowie, daughter of the Maori Princess Ono whose portrait hung in the old Art Gallery: "She was so dignified—and adventurous, when she was eighty-four she flew for the first time, down to the Bay of Plenty for a tribal meeting about land."

In those days, the village rang with home-made music. The Liedertafel choir sang on Mrs Macky's big verandah overlooking Cheltenham Beach: "People listened from the croquet lawns, or in boats; the garden was illuminated", according to a Macky daughter.

Cheerful choruses rang out from the beach also, when wives and children from "Soldiers' Row" joined their men for picnic teas after work. Miss Bessie Stewart of the Presbyterian church organised concerts. The Bartleys held musical evenings in their Victoria Road house, and so did Mrs Armstrong ("Aunt Angela" to many) in her Albert Road home. Miss Mary Mays and the French consul's wife were noted pianists. Such local talent was called upon in the 1914 War to entertain patients in the Convalescent Home at the top of Jubilee Avenue, and for music at balls and dances. These were formal affairs: "Invitation was by cards on which the chaperones were named". Liquor was banned; one unfortunate girl, having "had a beer with the boys", was never invited again.

All the big houses had croquet and tennis lawns on which ladies played. Mrs Doris Hutchison has only lately given up the game at the age of eighty-five. Sports clubs were then social centres. In Stanley Bay, still so rural that Kath Lund remembers seeing larks' nests on the turf when she walked with her father, the reclamation provided ground and "an old tin shed", where the Ngataringa Bay Tennis Club was founded by Mrs Pollard and others. "Everyone brought a plate on Saturday afternoons for concerts and dances where one provided one's own music". Golf on the Alison racecourse was more tricky, since Narrow Neck was often under water. Nora Whitley's father provided floating golf balls; Mrs Fisher remembers having to play in gumboots.

The 1918 influenza epidemic probably impressed the children more than the faraway war that preceded it. They were made to inhale burning sulphur put on shovels; saw people wearing masks in the streets; and could hardly help hearing talk of bodies being carted away. A group of women took soup to stricken families; many others enrolled as sorely-needed nurses. After the war, the village gained a midwife, Sister Jessie Milne. "With unfailing love and attention," says Mrs Emirali, "she delivered thousands of Devonportians into this world" at her two hospitals, "Cotswold" and "Pentlands", which were renowned throughout Auckland.

Also well-known after the 1914 War were two "Mothers of the Fleet" who befriended Navy "boys". One of them, "Ma" Burrows, had the rare distinction of being buried, when her time came, with full military honours.

In the Depression no-one starved in a place where "there were always fish to be caught with a bent nail and a bit of string". But many mothers were glad of the money brought in by children who mowed lawns at threepence a time; delivered milk and papers, collected grass seed or scrap metal on North Head; or swept the cinema floor, ankle-deep in peanut shells.

In World War II the Women's War Service Auxiliary under Miss Kay Rains made camouflage nets; helped at the Church Army Post; held Saturday sales of home-made goods, sewed and knitted busily. Mrs Poole remembers ferry trips to town laden with a child in a pushchair and a bundle of finished garments, collecting a big parcel of wool for more garments, and coming back the same way.

All this was traditional women's work, taken for granted. But now nothing can be taken for granted. Though Devonport still keeps much of its "island village" character, woman's place in it has changed.

Sister Brown on the lawn at Cotswold Hospital, which was used as a maternity home. *Alexander Turnbull Library*

Women for Peace march to the Naval Base gates on 24 May 1983. *John Miller*

CHANGES

In the last century, 92 per cent of Devonport women were listed as "independent" and the few women working did so in unskilled jobs. Though by 1909 some were clerks, bookbinders, nurses and telephonists, their children now recall them as housewives and homebodies. Most are still housewives, but few stay at home; they work in a variety of jobs and professions, as well as in the community.

Some whose mothers and grandmothers "left politics to the men" are now deeply involved. Since 1947 there have been ten women Councillors, two of them topping the poll for deputy mayor. All political parties now depend largely on women workers, and not only when the whistle blows and someone has to make the tea. Local education is no longer dominated by men: three of our schools have, or have had, women principals. Mothers control play-schools and kindergartens: they also run the community house, Wikitoria. The Library shows the trend clearly. For years it was administered by men, with a team of devoted volunteer women. Then in 1954 it acquired a professional Librarian, Miss Sadie Palmer (later Mrs W.A.L. Chapman). Under her guidance and that of Miss Helen Kennedy, membership is now over two-thirds of the population. Many are children, who use it with easy confidence. Based on the library were the Devonport Arts Festivals, in which another woman, Shirley Brickell, was responsible for organising much Maori participation, and gave us a chance to see Mrs Rangimarie Hetet and Mrs Hoeft at work on traditional Maori weaving. As Sir Bernard Fergusson said, such festivals "presented the Maori way of life as part of the North Shore life-pattern".

Devonport is now more full of home-made arts and crafts than home-made music, and many practitioners are women. In that building on the waterfront where the tea-rooms stood—where "upstairs you could sit and look at the harbour, and downstairs could leave the pram while doing a big of shopping", a woman potter works. A woman painter has enlivened an old wall in Rattray Street with a mural celebrating a child's delight in the waterfront: sea, seagulls, boats, and skies forever blue.

A tally of employed women in 1890 ends on a note of astonishment: "*One* accountant". This would hardly surprise anyone now, when businesswomen are taken for granted. So, too, are women photographers such as Ramai Hayward and Mrs Brash, who so lovingly recorded much of old Devonport before it vanished. There are also newspaperwomen. Hedda Bryson edited the *New Zealand Woman's Weekly* when it was started in Devonport's Fleet Street, and editor Pat Gundry has kept our local paper open for free discussion over many stirring years.

On a domestic note, women now drive our buses, tie up our ferries, deliver our mail, and those cheerful Garden Girls keep our flowerbeds blooming. There is also a crowd of anonymous women who all helped to make Devonport. In the early days, ships arriving from Home brought many single females, some subsidised by a Government desperate for women settlers. Many were snapped up on the wharf as wives: many found work as servants, and later, as housekeepers. Mrs Macky had a housekeeper at Cheltenham; so, too, did Dr Bennett in his big house near Melrose. Later refined into lady helps, or mother's helps, they kept many a home going but stay nameless—they were doing nothing spectacular. Also nameless is the resident who left £500 in her will for a covered gateway to O'Neill's cemetery: but "the Council never put in the gate".

Did the "first woman ever to cast a vote" do so in Devonport? No, but the first New Zealand woman voter might well have voted here.

The *Kestrel* heads towards Devonport, with Westhaven and the harbour bridge in the background. *Chris Miller*

Devonport Today

Molly G. Elliott
Photographs by Chris Miller

Walking from Cheltenham round to Devonport, I always cut across the vacant section at the corner of Cheltenham Road and King Edward Parade. At the turn of the century, my maternal grandparents lived there in a sprawling beige house with a verandah across its front. It had little architectural or historical significance, and came down years ago. Nothing has replaced it; a few cars park there.

My grandfather, David R.S. Galbraith, assayer and analytical chemist, obtained steel from ironsand in 1904. Many years ahead of his time and hopelessly impractical, he went broke. He would probably still recognise many of the houses. Indeed, the homes of children with whom my mother played still stand on King Edward Parade and in Victoria Road. So does the original St Leo's Convent, which she attended briefly—a strange choice for the daughter of a rigid Edinburgh Presbyterian. Of course, she could not possibly have attended Devonport School in that class-conscious time.

Old and new co-exist amicably in a borough where change occurs neither quickly nor disruptively; yet I miss the silhouette of the old gasometer that created a focal point for my windows. The pottery, though, makes a pleasant contribution to the long scatter of Albert Road and the lights of Melrose. That panorama embodies a lot of Devonport history: North Head, Mt Victoria, Stanley Point and nearby, the Waitemata golf links and immaculate fairways. I remember it as a racecourse, and I recall the accident which killed leading jockey Keith Voitre and closed the course fifty years ago.

Close at hand, the claystore, derelict for many years, now houses a workshop where enterprising people recondition engines, build boats, pot and weld, and perhaps discover themselves. This revitalisation typifies Devonport's talent for turning the old to modern use. Similarly, the Wikitoria Community Centre has evolved from the old headquarters of the wartime 15th AA Regiment, of which my uncle was OC. The old building now resounds to the voices of those

Left: Wikitoria Community House, Devonport. *Chris Miller*

Right: The gasometers before their demolition in March 1983. *North Shore Times Advertiser*

studying the guitar or drama, venturing on yoga or Maori, reducing their weight or the problems of women, and shows that people in Devonport need not be bored or isolated.

Looking out to Mt Victoria, as I often do, I see people on the top admiring the magnificent view—east to the Coromandel and west to the Waitakeres and over the Waitemata Harbour and the city. Sometimes I plod up there myself, remembering the days when we girls from Belmont School attended "Tech" on the lower slopes, ostensibly learning to cook, to the scorn of our mothers. Like the original primary school, the "Tech" has long gone from Mt Victoria but a handsome new building has replaced it. Few children in the world have a finer site or a more splendid outlook. From here you can look down into the Sunday-silent side streets and along the sweep of King Edward Parade. For years people have forseen that the waterfront might eventually resemble Kirribilli with apartment blocks ousting the old houses. So far this has happened only on a modest scale. Devonport does not rush into things—and is none the worse for that.

Devonport sets great store by the past, as witness streets of Victorian villas in Melrose. Sturdy, durable houses, they date from the early days of Pakeha settlement. Their sound construction, excellent building material and conscientious maintenance make them good for another century, but the original owners might be shocked at their often vivid colours. By contrast, Tainui Road presents a spectrum from massive Victorian residences to the compact bow-windowed style of the 1920s.

All houses, regardless of age, have gardens fore and aft. Nowhere is the New Zealand tradition of "a little bit of ground with a fence

Devonport has always had a talent for adapting old buildings for modern use.

Above left: A soldier's cottage. *Chris Miller*
Above right: 90 Victoria Rd. *Chris Miller*
Below: The front of the old Presbyterian Church became the Devonport Museum,
the back a private home *(Left) Chris Miller*

Out and about on the streets of Devonport. *Chris Miller*

all round" more stoutly defended than in such old-established places. Devonport has also retained its trees, not only natives but deciduous exotics. In the exultant foliage of high summer, they flourish among houses and along streets. Devonport "village" has some of the finest— towering palms, spreading Moreton Bay figs with high-arched, sinister roots, and pohutukawas that look like crimson cauliflowers when they burst into Christmas bloom.

Most shops are individually owned and perpetuate the idea of shopping as a friendly conversation rather than an encounter with a computer. In turn Devonport appreciates the charm of its Victorian premises. Most of the original facades have been retained, and in the newly-opened arcades and courts, old bricks, ripened in patches to near-purple, have been harmoniously used. The pleasant little shops tempt you off the street into quiet byways.

ROUND TRIP
PASSENGERS
FROM
DEVONPORT
MUST
DISEMBARK
& PURCHASE
TICKETS AT
AUCKLAND

INTENDING PASSENGERS PLEASE
KEEP CLEAR OF GANGWAY
UNTIL PASSENGERS HAVE DISEMBARKED

Walking home. *Chris Miller*

On the hottest day a breeze whips off the harbour and across Marine Square, from which you can glimpse the harbour bridge. No-one would question the benefits it brings, but many still prefer the relaxing ferry crossing. With coffee bars, restaurants and upholstered seats, the ferries have smartened up; so have the buses in their new Antwerp blue livery and their trim blue-shirted drivers. Yet some may remember with nostalgia more casual days when one driver might call, "Don't run for the bus, love. Just give me a wave and I'll stop," or another duck home for a quick cup of tea on a blustery night.

There is still little traffic on the side-streets, but on Lake Road with its three switchbacks swooping up and downhill on the way to Takapuna, things are more energetic. In days before the bridge it boasted New Zealand's heaviest volume of traffic, and though that record has long gone to the Hutt motorway, there is still plenty of movement on Lake Road. And wherever you go, at whatever hour, joggers pound the pavement.

A child's-eye view of an old gun emplacement on Mt Victoria. *Chris Miller*

It seems incongruous that so peaceful a spot should have such strong ties with the armed services. It even saw its share of Maori battles in pre-Pakeha times. From Mt Victoria you look down on the naval dockyard with its grey frigates alongside. The former Ventnor Hotel has become the WREN's headquarters. The naval houses on Ngataringa Road, the establishment on North Head, HMS *Tamaki* and the army's Fort Cautley overlooking Narrow Neck—all stress this service tradition, which invades my kitchen when an easterly carries the sound of the band's burnished brass from morning parade. Both North Head and Mt Victoria have always been natural strong points, as the remains of guns and searchlight emplacements show. Braced to do so much, and luckily, called on to do so little, they commanded Rangitoto Channel and the harbour approaches during World War II. Now the radar station stands where the old Mt Victoria signal mast once raised its cones and balls to announce shipping movements. The local folk music club has converted a bunker to its headquarters.

It blows fiercely up there. When a tiny pohutukawa was planted in memory of Prime Minister Norman Kirk, one wondered if the poor thing would survive. But survive it has, and grown into a sturdy shrub likely to spread beyond its white picket fence. It looks down on the ferries on which "Big Norm" once worked.

Overseas visitors familiar with the gross commercialisation of European beaches are mystified by our refusal to get above ourselves. Why don't we line our beaches with hotels and outdoor restaurants? We prefer to enjoy them as they are, by swimming, sunbathing, running, windsurfing, picnicking in shorts and floppy sunhats, all for free. One can only imagine what such "development" would do to Narrow Neck's little promenade where generations of yachties got their first boating experience, or to nearby Woodall Park (which commemorates a former mayor), where you may picnic, play football or cricket, and sometimes go to a circus. More spacious Cheltenham, with its gardens running down to the beach, might suffer even worse. Now, even on fine winter days, you can find someone enjoying the

The southern end of Cheltenham Beach and the eastern reaches of North Head. *Chris Miller*

beach, perhaps a Maori family gathering cockles at low tide out on the glistening mud, or kids building a driftwood fire to cook vulcanised eggs and charred bacon. On such a day and at such an age, it tastes delectable in this setting.

Some things change little, though a decade ago Woodall Park consisted of little more than a grassed stretch adjacent to the golf links. It is a pity that its clearance has meant the disappearance of the pheasants that used to whirr out of the scrub, but larks still spiral up. People feed the ducks that make their home along the banks of the creek and on the little island. A kindly notice on the road warns, "Beware! Ducks crossing". You can hear a magpie's chuckle, watch the swallows' darting flight, glimpse a white-faced heron and listen to mynahs denouncing each other. Spring sometimes brings a tui to garden kowhais and the massive flame tree growing among the

A glassblower at work at The Works. *Chris Miller*

bamboo which fills the former clay pit. Here the brickmaker's tiny cottage still stands, as it has done for over a century, at the corner of Lake Road and Hanlon Crescent.

Flowers and trees are everywhere. Kowhais and pohutukawas, roses and bougainvillea, hibiscus and camellias, honeysuckle along fences— all create exotic illusions of the tropics. They enhance the charm of the old houses, decorated with finials and wooden lace in rigid white swags. Most of these have been restored to their original elegance in streets running to the beach, where ships seem to pass perilously close to the shore and yachts ghost past North Head. Many of these houses have arrogant little towers, perhaps aping English grandeur or perhaps simply as lookouts for incoming ships.

Devonport has long been interested in the arts. For some years it acted as the focal point of the North Shore Arts Festival, with concerts on the reserve hard by the excellent library. A little way up the street the Compendium Gallery offers distinguished exhibits of contemporary painting, weaving, jewellery and pottery, inviting people in by its easy casualness. Along the waterfront near the Masonic Tavern (over a hundred years old and still popular) is the complex called simply The Works, where you can watch the glass-blower and the potters and the painter, and buy what pleases you. Just up Church Street hiding inside what was once a volcanic cone, is the recently organised museum, full of old photographs, ancient machinery, an enormous dray, and lots of sentiment.

More than anywhere else, King Edward Parade exemplifies Devonport's yachting traditions. Boats up for maintenance at the Yacht Club thrust their bows to the pavement; others swing at moorings off Duder's Beach, by Victoria Wharf, and in Stanley Bay. Along the foreshore, over a century ago, some of Auckland's first boatbuilders operated their yards with slipways sloping down to the handy beaches.

These beaches still draw devotees. At all seasons they come—family parties, lone wolves, couples, and groups of small boys on foot or bike (or in yacht-length cars). Some come efficiently equipped with meticulous hampers, some make do with plastic bags, hold-alls, parcels

The Masonic Tavern and Watson Memorial Clock, from North Head. *Chris Miller*

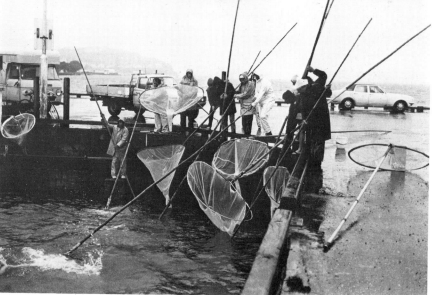

or buckets for the catch, which may amount to little more than a pakete or two like parings of tin. If they come by ferry they tend to settle down on Devonport Beach itself, or the nearby reserve. In summer, when a concave swell of sand surfaces near the wharf, daring youngsters dive joyously from the piles, careful not to disturb the serious fishermen. These anglers assemble like the final chorus of a musical comedy. Some prop their rods against the stringers like the Queen laying a wreath, others perch on the foundations of the old ferry gangway, alert for whitebait. There they lunge and plunge, scooping their outsize nylon nets as if pursuing marine butterflies through the tide.

Across the square, in sharp contrast, the Esplanade Hotel displays its embellishments of gold on white, and guests behind wide landsape windows gaze at the harbour view and at the flowers which front the library and encircle the memorial to the dead of World War I. Those of World War II are commemorated in the avenue of trees, pohutukawas and Norfolk pines, further up the main road.

Top: Fishing off Victoria Wharf in 1938. *Auckland Star.*
Bottom: Whitebaiting from the vehicular ferry wharf in 1982. *Ron Johnson*

Devonport's affinity with the sea is recorded in the large mural recently painted in recollection of the artist's own childhood on a wall at the corner of Rattray Street, and another on the bright walls of the Wikitoria Community Centre, where a ferry seems to be sailing down the street. The best place to see the ships is, of course, North Head. Most of the population gather here for the regatta on Anniversary Day, or for the start of the Auckland-Mar del Plata leg of the Whitbread Round-the-world yacht race. At other times, the Royal Yacht *Britannia* or the *QE2*, or a visiting warship, with or without protesters, glides into the harbour. Some of the tracks round North Head follow the old Maori ditch and palisade defence, in part obliterated by wild cinerarias and periwinkles. A later defence was mounted in World War II by the 9th Coastal Regiment, as a plaque duly records. Much of the defences are underground. You can wander through the resonant tunnels, torch in hand, and even inspect the famous "disappearing gun", a 40-ton, 8-inch breach loader, which recoiled underground for reloading. This monster was to defend us against the nineteenth-century Russian invaders. Above ground you may finger the 9th Regiment's Memorial Saluting Battery of 8 kg field guns, honouring the men who guarded the harbour entrance in World War II. These guns point out over Torpedo Bay and the pilot wharf, home of the *Aucklander*.

On a still day you can hear voices on deck as the ships steal out under the shadow of North Head, and feel your heart lift as a frigate departs with its crew, in a high state of polish, lined up at stations for leaving harbour. Sometimes incoming ships anchor off Stanley Bay, probably the quietest part of Devonport (although glorious with fire-engines at its junction with Victoria Road). Calliope Road threads its way along the crest, exhibiting the usual mix of houses, new and old. The Naval Commander enjoys a splendid Victorian mansion, and an old two-storey house has been converted into an excellent restaurant. Stanley Bay itself is a sort of crimp in the peninsula, separating the rest of the borough from the rather superior enclave on Stanley Point, lush with wistaria and magnolias. Devon Park, one of Auckland's first tower blocks, lifts the wide windows of its apartments into the path of the south-west winds. As yet, no other tower blocks have followed to set a local fashion.

Wandering round the streets, chatting to friendly people, absorbing the panoramas from the high points or merely loafing along the waterfront, you understand why people love Devonport.

A view from North Head of the controversial visit of the USS *Texas* on 2 August 1983. *John Miller*

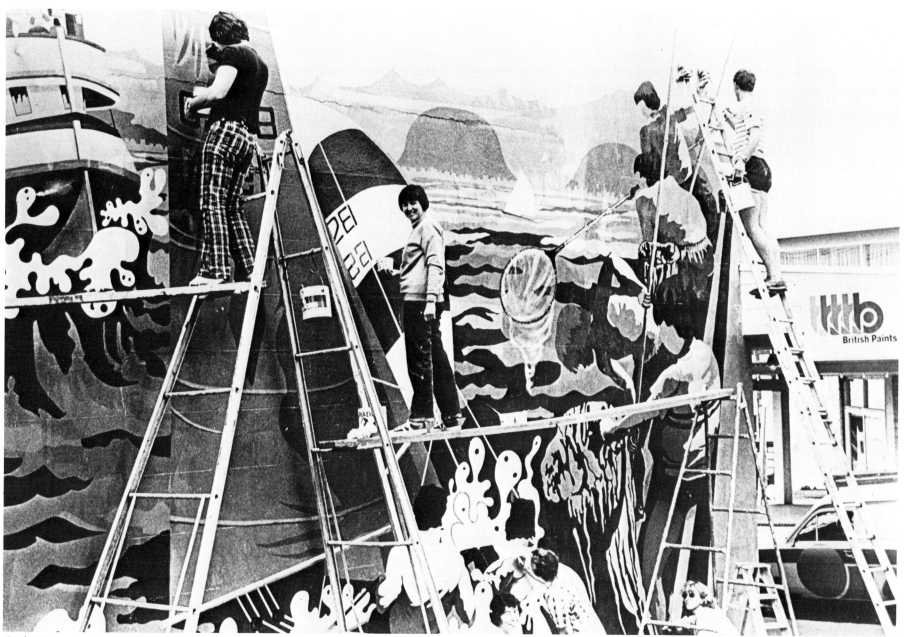

Gael O'Leary at work on her Rattray St mural in 1983. *North Shore Times Advertiser*

A view of Mt Victoria from Harry Cobley's residence in Cheltenham Road, 1873. *Auckland Public Library*

A Chronology of the Borough Council

First Territorial District proclaimed (County of Eden) 1842
Six parishes proclaimed for land registration (Takapuna)
Six "HUNDREDS" created (Pupuke) 1848 (to 1860)
Provincial Council established 1853 (to 1877)
Flagstaff Highway District formed 1866 (to 1886)

FLAGSTAFF HIGHWAY DISTRICT BOARD

1867
February 25: First meeting of those claiming right to vote. First rate struck—½d in the pound.
April 1: First bylaw passed (not valid).
July 3: Collector of rates appointed. First officer of the Board.
September 11: Meeting to inspect roads.
October 1: Annual meeting—rate set at 1d in the pound.

1868
March 17: Board resigns in protest that Flagstaff has not been proclaimed. Proposed by Colonel Wynyard that the Board cease its activities until October 1868.
October 6: Censure proposed by ratepayers to Board for not collecting rates withdrawn.
November 10: Valuation of properties.
December 3: Request to Superintendent to alter name to Devonport Highway Board.

1869
February 5: Board protests at interference of Provincial Government with public roads.
March 15: Constable appointed.
April 13: First public works proceeded with.

August 12: Dog Nuisance Act in force. Request from Mr Cobley to sink wells on Lake Road (Church Street) and give one for public use. Public meeting called for parents interested in establishing a Boys Common School.
October 23: Appointment of a Ranger to administer Thistle Act, Weeds and Watercourses Act and cattle regulations.

1870
May 30: Beginning of work on Beach Road (King Edward Parade) to North Head—beginning of problem with E. Alison over stone wall, was to be Council's biggest lawsuit—total cost £800.
October 25: Application to Commissioner of Crown Lands for use of lands for ratepayers (first move to obtain reserves in the area).
December 1: Superintendent refuses to hand over reserves.
December 30: Request to Superintendent that Flagstaff Hill be placed in the hands of the Trustees for grazing.

1871
February 14: Superintendent says would not interfere, to ask Lessee T. Duder.
April 5: Discovery of scoria deposits behind Presbyterian Church—application to Superintendent to quarry.
September 19: Cattle regulations adopted 21 September 1869 now put in force to combat straying cattle.

1872
June 24: Considered laying down iron pipes in Anne St—first real attempt at drainage—decided against due to cost.
November 21: Oliver Mays granted permission to erect a verandah.

1873
January 14: Holmes given permission to build a steamer on the beach—beginning of ship building activity on the foreshore.
February 3: Move to impound horses—previously ran free.
February 19: Secretary of Crown Lands offers Flagstaff Hill (Mt Victoria) to Board.
April 8: T. Duder asked to remove cattle from Flagstaff Hill—Board would make over some of the land for grazing.
September 15: Special constable granted to area.

1874
August 13: Grant of £50 from Provincial Treasurer for trees on hill. Tree planting on Victoria Road near Naval Reserve.
November 1: Appointment of Engineer to the Board—commission on work done.

1876
February 9: Case of typhoid fever reported—resolved to request proclamation of the Board as local Board of Health.

1877
January 15: Sanitary inspector appointed under Public Health Act 1876.
May 1: Board receives first health report—decision to enforce earth closet system in more populous streets.
September 24: Constable made Inspector of Nuisance (1876 Public Health Act).

1878
March 13: North Head jurisdiction given to Waitemata County Council. Board receives grazing rights.
July 10: Acquisition of three foreshore reserves for bathing. Free library formed (first in Auckland Provincial District).

Alexander Alison and his wife Jane. They settled on the Devonport foreshore in 1854. *Dr A. Armitage*

1879
February 10: One of Trustees elected to Harbour Board.
April 15: Management of North Head handed over to Board.
July 28: Annual meeting—protest to Harbour Board to prevent disenfranchisement of Devonport Highways Board and Petition to acquire Triangle under Public Reserves Act.

1880
March 8: Weekly rate levied for removal of nightsoil.
July 15: Small fee to be charged for library use.

Albert Road at Church St, c.1880. *Devonport School Album*

1881

January 8: Control of Flagstaff Hill and Devonport Domain handed over to Devonport and Mt Victoria Domain Board.

August 2: Contribution of £1 given to petition requesting abolition of Waitemata City Council.

September 12: Prohibition on the keeping of pigs.

1882

April 17: Protest (to O. Mays) re Auckland Harbour Board abandoning the Devonport Wharf.

June 6: Six lamps bought for street lighting.

December 22: Petition to Board (46 signatures) requesting a special meeting to discuss Highway Board becoming a Borough.

1883

May 14: Seal ordered—common seal approved by Government.

May 23: Scoria reserve vested.

June 13: Membership on Board extended from five to nine.

August 13: Streets to be 1 chain wide, formed and channelled before being taken over.

September 10: Request from Devonport Steam Ferry Co to lay tram tracks with exclusive rights. Bylaws drawn up.

1884

February 11: Naval Triangle vested in Board.

March 10: Committee set up to consider question of becoming a Borough.

July 14: 100 Trees ordered from Auckland Domain for Triangle.

1885

February 9: Auckland Harbour Board proposes reclamation of Shoal Bay—east side of Lake Road. Inspection proposed of Lake Takapuna (Pupuke) as a water supply.

May 11: Board's solicitors instructed to draw up a petition under the Municipal Corporations Act for formation into a Borough. New cemetery gazetted.

May: Applied to House of Representatives for a regular policeman and the construction of a gaol.

August 10: County Council notifies intention to lay a rate of ¾d in the pound. Board to resist.

November 16: Request for three fire bells as brigade being formed.

1886

February 9: Petition for proclamation as Borough sent.

May 6: Gazetted as Borough.

June 28: Accounts turned over to Devonport Borough Council.

DEVONPORT BOROUGH COUNCIL

1886

May 5: Devonport Borough gazetted.

June 14: First meeting of Devonport Borough Council.

July 12: Borough seal purchased for £10.

September 6: First bylaws adopted—licensing and control of slaughterhouses, control of swimming.

October 25: Recommended that the Finance and Legal committee prepare a petition to have borough boundaries extended to low water mark.

November 22: Request for a report on taking the Triangle under the Public Works Act as a site for public building.

December 29: Under-secretary General of the General Crown Lands Office notifies Council that under 1882 Cemeteries Act no new cemetery can be established in the Borough.

1887

January 10: Petition to Governor for extension of boundaries signed and sealed.

March 1: Council decides to purchase sections at Hurstmere (edge of Lake Takapuna—Pupuke—) for waterworks scheme.

March 14: Section at Hurstmere bought.

March 31: New Borough boundaries gazetted. Tenders called for new Council Chambers.

May 23: Council decides to look for cemetery lands outside the district raising money in security of Lot 1 (unused cemetery).

June 27: Council meets for first time in new chambers. Hurstmere section (for waterworks) sold.

August 18: Waterworks committee recommends no action over water supply due to cost.

September 5: After a public meeting the Council resolves to take action over water supply.

1888

February 2: Council again defers water supply.

April 16: Formal demand from Waitemata County Council for £300 compensation for cemetery.

September 3: Council votes to take legal action over Alison's wall encroachment.

1889

January 19: £300 paid to Waitemata County for cemetery.

Calliope dry dock under construction in 1887. *Auckland Public Library*

April 1: Set as day for formal process of removing Alison's wall.

April 6: Alison threatens contractors.

June 10: Chief surveyor for Auckland refuses to be involved in conflict. 100 Macrocarpa trees ordered for cemetery reserve.

1890

March 17: Agreement from Auckland Harbour Board to deal with dead animals washed up on the beach.

May 27: Deputation from District Schools committee for help in obtaining extra land from the Mt Victoria Domain Board.

August 4: Rangitoto Island brought under Public Domains Act. Governor's powers delegated to Corporation as the Rangitoto Island Domain Board.

August 18: Council adopts conciliatory approach with Navy over the Triangle.

October 27: Auditor-General wishes to know why Council purchased new cemetery.

November 11: Mistake in gazetting closure of burial grounds. Deed being prepared conveying part of Shoal Bay reclamation from the Auckland Harbour Board.

December 12: Annual meeting—Niccol notes that Borough acquired 110 acres as endowments and an equitable right in Rangitoto.

1891

June 8: E.W. Alison tries to get postal charges reduced.

August 31: Solicitor's opinion on legality of cemetery purchase forwarded to Auditor-General.

November 11: Protest from Lake deputation over sending fever patients from borough to the Lake district. Letter from W.J. Napier re water supply—first of many.

December 3: Deputation from the Lake to discuss a proposed tramway scheme to connect the two areas.

1892

January 18: Auditor-General disallows loan raised for cemetery—liable to legal proedings.

January 26: Special meeting over water supply—agree that Lake Takapuna is the only source.

February 24: Notice of intention to raise a special loan of £15,000 published.

March 14: Solicitors advise purchasing of land at Lake Takapuna.

April 7: Poll taken over question of loan—vote to proceed.

May 9: Terms set for water supply design.

August 15: Council buys land on Lake Takapuna.

September 26: Protest from Lake Takapuna residents over taking of water—solicitors recommend a test case.

October 24: Certificate of title received for Lot 1 (Cemetery) and reclaimed land on Shoal Bay from Auckland Harbour Board.

November 8: Well sunk at Lake.

1893

April 10: Major lending institutions not keen to lend at less than 6 per cent. Council decides to raise loan on debentures at 5½ per cent.

June 8: £15,028.12.6 raised for loan.

June 22: Oliver Mays opposed to purchase of pump engine. Beginning of increasingly vocal opposition.

1894

June 25: Auckland Harbour Board Empowerng Act passed conveying the Triangle to the Council.

August 11: Official opening of Devonport water supply.

1895

October 24: Council calls for designs for a drainage scheme. Decides not to grant money to E.W. Alison for services as Mayor.

1896

March 16 Council requests a summary of voting rights from the Borough's Solicitors.

May 29: Trees to be planted in the Triangle, naval depot reserve and opposite Lot 15a (Alison's).

Nothing happened on this site in 1887, and doesn't seem to have happened up to the date of this photograph, 1983. *North Shore Times Advertiser*

December: Oliver Mays withdraws from the Mayoralty contest.

1897

January 19: Deadlock over candidate for the Harbour Board exposes two factions in Council.

February 11: Council fails to elect a member for Board—Government takes over appointment.

March 10: Decision to have the library closed and books disposed of.

August: W.J. Napier objects to Council giving permission to resident to construct drain outlet on Cheltenham Beach. Brings drainage question to a head.

September: M. Niccol stands for Council and fails.

1898

February 23: M. Niccol elected to Auckland Harbour Board.

June 8: Arbor Day on Rangitoto Island—Council has exotic plants established. Controversy over role of Rangitoto as a recreation area.

June 21: Council refuses to allow building on the naval reserve (Windsor Reserve).

June 26: Council decides to put J. Macky (Mayor) forward for Harbour Board before M. Niccol's term has expired.

September 6: M. Niccol stands for Council—conflict with Oliver Mays over performance of Council.

September 7: Niccol beats Mays for seat on Council.

October 12: Joseph Macky asked to stand as Mayor again.

A day at the races, 1908. *Devonport School Album*

Coronation festivities on 9 August 1902, when King Edward VII finally came to the throne. *David Barratt*

November: Devonport Borough Council offers to supply water to Northcote and Birkenhead.

1899

February 14: Joseph Macky voted to represent the Council on Harbour Board. Niccol edged out. Council decided to ask for a £17,500 loan at 4 per cent.

February 15: Special meeting held by Takapuna/Birkenhead residents to protest the Council's move to supply sole right to water.

March 25: Successful poll taken for loan. Municipal Franchise Act passed – entitles anyone paying rent of more than £10 to be on the electors roll. Both husband and wife can be on roll, and leaseholders.

August 16: Beginning of conflict over the Mt Victoria and Devonport Domain Board.

September 5: E.W. Alison, Robert Logan and James Dunning elected to Council. Dunning and Alison often in conflict.

1900

January 3: Council discussed the possibility of acquiring Mt Cambria, loan of £3,500.

January 26: Councillor proposes £25 vote for town hall design – deferred. Mt Cambria bought without reference to ratepayers.

April 19: Council issues a request to people to lay poison for rats (poison available from Council) – bubonic plague scare.

July 8: Council considers a further loan of £8,000 to extend and complete drainage, repair roads and to buy Mt Cambria.

September 6: Dr Laing asked to stand for Mayor. Deputation includes J. Macky, sitting Mayor.

1901

January 18: Devonport branch of Auckland Savings Bank opened.

February 6: Devonport Ferry Co and Council meet. Company agrees to increase trips and reduce yearly ticket costs. Niccol asked to stand for Mayor. Alison decides to withdraw.

June 18: Slaughtering campaign against rats. Public Health Department wants to know how many killed – 500.

June 24: Number of staff to be reduced due to debts of Council.

July 25: Notice that domains to be vested in Council to operate as Domain Board.

October 30: Northcote and Birkenhead residents propose own water supply.

November 27: C.C. Dacre proposes a band rotunda to be built on Windsor Reserve.

1902

March 5: Request for permission to remove the old Flagstaff hotel. Deputation from football club to ask for permission to build a shed on Devonport Domain.

April 17: Malcolm Niccol leaving the area because of duties as Grandmaster of the Freemasons.

May 25: Council decides to have a house-to-house inspection to check on rats. E.W. Alison to stand for Mayor.

September: Request from Christchurch Borough Council for information about the unimproved rating system (Devonport was the first to adopt it).

1903
April 8: Notification to Council from Harbour Board that no sewage to be drained into the harbour.
April 29: Oliver Mays dies.
May 27: Takapuna Racing Club wants to lease land leased by Duder brothers from Auckland Harbour Board.
June 4: Fountain erected in memory two men killed in Boer War.

1904
March: Debate over the merits of the unimproved rating system. Poll taken over valuation system—poll negative.

1905
March 7: Official opening of the new water works.

1907
January 17: Application to Council to remove Presbyterian church from Church Street to burial grounds, corner Victoria and Albert Roads.

February 11: Council is given permission to use prison labour on the Devonport Domain. Treasury loan of £1300 to complete drainage and £5700 to extend water mains received.
April 9: Alison declines to stand again as Mayor due to duties as Member of Parliament.
April 23: Council protests the Harbour Board forcing them to give up their supply of water to shipping. Council writes to chief gaoler for prisoners to work on domains.
May 7: W.J. Napier objects to removal of shells

from Admiralty reserve—told by Council they intend to grass the area. Deputation to Council for a technical school deferred for 12 months.
September 24: Council declines Auckland Harbour Board offer for land near Stanley Bay for a morgue.
October 8: Mt Cambria leased for grazing.
December 3: Auckland Gas Co. refuses to hand over lighting of lamps to Council.

1908
February 26: Council decides to instruct

The Great White Fleet in all its glory in 1908. A panorama by H. Winkelmann. *Auckland Institute and Museum*

solicitors to prepare a bill to municipalise gas supply. Charles Savage resigns as Foreman of Works (30 years). Application by E.J. Fenn to have sole right to supply electricity.

April: Council decides not to consider matter of electricity.

June 3: Deputation from Takapuna to have Council reconsider water metering outside borough.

July 15: Request to have tramway option given to Devonport Transport Company.

August 28: Devonport Post Office opened.

1909

April 5: Devonport Ratepayers Association (recently formed) present 'ticket' for forthcoming election.

April 10: Devonport Golf Club applies to lease the cemetery reserve.

April 21: Increased bitterness between some council members and Ratepayers Association. Thomas Considine and other councillors urge Government to establish worker's dwellings in Devonport. Borough loan dept £65,700. Criticism of the location of sewage pumping station on the Admir-

alty Reserve. Domain leased to Rugby Union – Council becomes involved in debate over amateur and professional football.

October 20: Council is condemned for running Council herds on Devonport Domain.

November 3: Decision made to proceed with the building of a recreation reserve on Rangitoto. Devonport Borough Council decides to content itself with maintenance of borough and not to embark on major schemes.

1910

January 19: Decision to request a loan for £33,200 – largest amount of £10,910 to go on roads, brings strong criticism of Council's handling of money. Poll passes loans for manual training school, drainage of Victoria Park, £1000 for Stanley Park, morgue and reservoir.

June 10: Council opposes attempt by the Marine Department to take over ferry licences from the Auckland Harbour Board.

October 6: Pressure from ratepayers for

conveniences on Cheltenham Beach. Growing debate in Council over state of roads.

November 3: Council shows disinterest in engineers' report of increasingly outdated water supply.

December 8: Council diverts money for roads from water works account. Increasing debate over council's ability to handle finance—demand for a comprehensive programme. Question of town clock deferred until after election.

1911

March 28: Ewen Alison declines to stand as mayor. Handley elected unopposed.

May 25: Question of reopening of Devonport wharf raised. Minister of Internal Affairs says construction of a sea wall is not a suitable coronation monument—Council decide to proceed anyway.

1912

April 4: Problem of control of Lake Takapuna. Waitemata County moves to take control— possible formation of a Water Board to prevent takeover. Water level of lake down four feet due to heavy consumption.

April 24: Work begins on tea kiosk (completed July 1913). Application to Rangitoto Domain Board to show films in caves Wednesdays, Saturdays and holidays, music by bagpipes and tin whistles. Council declines.

August 29: Protest meeting of Devonport, Birkenhead and Northcote over control of ferries.

October 3: Cr J. Allen threatens to resign over Cheltenham Beach. Waitemata Chamber of Commerce threatens an injunction against Council by Devonport people to stop removal of sand.

Swimming in the dry dock, c.1910.
Devonport Museum

Cheltenham Beach in 1913

A by no means too fanciful artist's impression of Cheltenham Beach which appeared in the *NZ Herald* on 2 March 1912. *Auckland Institute and Museum*

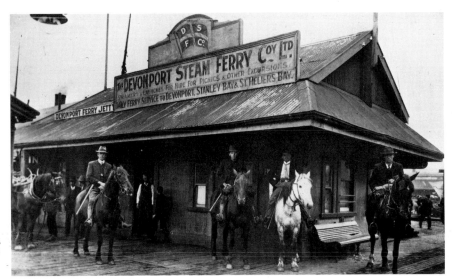

Farmers acting as mounted police during the 1913 waterfront strike. *Auckland Public Library*

King Edward Parade, c.1916

1913
January: Council asks for tenders for electricity supply.
December 13: Water Board to be created to control Lake Takapuna—five members including one from Crown Lands office. Proposal to erect Council chambers in conjunction with the Bank of New Zealand.

1914
May 5: J.C. Macky, ex-Mayor, drowned on the *Lusitania*.
June 10: Council moves to have a joint meeting with other marine boroughs to consider common interests.
August 3: Electricity Supply Corporation Ltd given option to supply electricity to the Borough. Water supply restrictions imposed by the Board of Control. Call services to be metered. Meeting of Borough Council to consider a Greater North Shore movement due to Auckland Harbour Board's intention to raise ferry charges to equate with the upkeep of wharves

July 8: Devonport asked to reduce water consumption by half; Control Board considers additional sources for supply.

1915
Consulting engineer classifies the Borough's roads into three divisions and notes terrible condition of all but a few.
June 20: Water supply almost finished.

1916
A.M. Pickford, newly elected Mayor, presents comprehensive programme including re-organisation of all council departments so more able to respond when loans available.
December 3: New Presbyterian church opened. 150 street lights installed.

1917
Sewage pumps electrified.

1918
Admiralty Reserve changed to Windsor Reserve. Old Flagstaff Reserve incorporated into recreation reserve.

1919
July 24: Council agrees to support a provincial War Memorial Museum.
August 14: Meeting over construction of a war memorial. Various proposals—memorial hall, reading room, municipal offices, Corinthian column, astronomical observatory, gymnasium, cottage hospital.
September 2: Discussion of alternative water supplies.
September 18: Water diviner called in—the Rev. H. Mason of Otahuhu says to abandon Mt Cambria and concentrate on Vauxhall Rd.

1920
July 29: Council refuses Defence Department request to Council to have drilling on Devonport Domain.
November 11: Deputation from "Devonport Good Roads Campaign Committee"—petition from 542 ratepayers asking for a roads loan.
November 16: Criticism of Council neglect of domains.

November 18: Deputation from fire brigade over need for a fire station.
December 16: Possiblity of setting up an electricity authority raised. Two German machine guns given to Borough as war trophies.
December 18: Marine Borough Association considers the formation of a Water Supply Board to supercede the Lake Takapuna Board of Control—problem of representation.

1921
January 13: Suggestion that the four boroughs should construct a central power station for five years until electricity is available from the city.
April 13: All but Birkenhead Borough in favour of an electric power board. Council considers proposal for a harbour bridge.
May 7: Criticism by ratepayers of Council's use of a water diviner.
August 8: New fire engine and equipment bought.

September 3: Proposal to buy 600 acres in Waitakeres as a watershed placed before marine boroughs.

October 31: Objections to disfigurement of Rangitoto where Council had been leasing allotments for revenue.

December 12: Meeting of all Auckland local authorities to deal with problem of rats.

1922

January 3: Council proposes to borrow £10,000 to pay loan of £10,000 taken out in 1900.

April 28: Meeting over water supply—possibility of a greater metropolitan supply system.

July 14: Purchase of Electricity Company confirmed by poll—£40,000.

August 31: Council proposes to concrete Church St and Vauxhall Rd rather than Cheltenham Beach route—accused of favouritism.

September: Appointment of honorary rangers to eradicate wallabies, rabbits, possums etc. from Rangitoto.

December 2: Strong warning against continued use of Lake Takapuna by the Department of Health. Board of Control recommends chlorinating plants rather than a new supply.

1923

March 22: Residents warned to boil water before drinking.

May: New Mayor says Council unwise in buying electricity supply. Consideration of supply scheme from Upper or Lower Wairau. Devonport opposed to a temporary scheme now that chlorination plant installed.

July 5: Seven councillors leave in protest at the Mayor's (Thomas Lamont) criticism of the Council—ostensible conflict over sale of electricity plant to the Waitemata Power Board. Special meeting of ratepayers calls on Councillors to resign.

Left: An aerial view of Devonport and North Head, taken from a 22 Flying School flying boat in 1921. An Avro 504K seaplane fills the top of the picture. *Auckland Public Library*

Right: Clean Up Week in August 1923. *Devonport Gazette*

December 10: First mention of Ngataringa Bay as a development area; idea of causeway to Bayswater.

1924

January 16: Takapuna, Birkenhead and Northcote to combine for a power board—no way of including Devonport with its own power supply.

April 9: Proposal to take water from Rangipuni stream near Albany—Health Department not in favour.

July 19: Gordon Coates, Minister of Public Works, refused to countenance a separate board or joining with Auckland City Power Board. Auckland Board would probably provide cheaper power.

September 4: Deputation from School Board and Chamber of Commerce press for a grammar school—400 school children commuting to the city.

1925

February 19: Council approaches the Minister of Justice about prisoners to be used on Rangitoto to construct road for tourists.

June 5: Ambulance located in Devonport.

June 23: Meeting to discuss formation of an Auckland Provincial Water Board to get water from Taupo. Auckland City Council in favour of Waitakeres.

July 29: Council decides to dispose of its electricity supply to Waitemata Power Board for £61,000.

August 13: Permission given to use prison labour on Rangitoto.

December 4: Council withdraws from Auckland Provincial Water Board scheme and consults Auckland City Council over Waitakeres.

1926

April 17: Opening of Takapuna Grammar School.

June 10: Authorisation for new wharf at Devonport from Auckland Harbour Board. Queens Parade to be improved at the same time.

1927

February 4: Question of a joint transport authority for four boroughs raised.

June 16: Increased retrenchment of Council—46 of 106 staff dispensed with. Many loans coming to maturity—Borough revenue exhausted.

July 25: Devonport electricity service only to be emergency—now lit by Auckland Horahora supply.

August 1: Mayor Aldridge opposed to amalgamation with other boroughs.

October 11: Four boroughs decide on Waitakere water supply scheme.

1928

February 9: Council apply for £12,000 unemployment loan—ratified 14 February. Lake Pupuke drops below sea level.

July 6: Opening of new ferry wharf.

Devonport United Band Xmas Statty 1929-30

All Proceeds in aid of Contest Fund

WINDSOR RESERVE.   DEVONPORT.

(Lent by kind permission of His Worship the Mayor, E. Aldridge Esq., and Councillors of Devonport Borough Council).

DECEMBER 23, 1929 to JANUARY 7, 1930.
DECEMBER 23 1929 to JANUARY 7, 1930.

MORNING, NOON AND NIGHT!
Both Days Inclusive.

MERRY-GO-ROUNDS — HOOP-LA — EGYPTIAN ILLUSIONS — KNOCK 'EM — SKITTLES — HORSE RACING IN MINIATURE — ROLL 'EM — JAZZING, ETC., ETC.

WE'RE HERE! BRING THE CHILDREN ALONG! IF YOU CANNOT GO FOR A HOLIDAY, SPEND IT WITH US! COUNCIL ATTRACTIONS ARE FREE, BUT THE STATTY JUST EXCHANGE THEIR ATTRACTIONS FOR A SMALL COIN! SOMEONE SAID A MILLION!

Safe Bathing—Good Punt—Plenty Shade—Glorious Views—No Stray Dogs—Dressing Sheds—No Noise or Bustle—Pleasant Neighbours—Plenty o' Fun—Amusements of all kinds—Nice Girls — Oh, BOY!

Top: Christmas Statty, 1929-30. *Devonport Borough Council*

Bottom: Devonport's budget for 1927-28. The borough's estimated annual income of £54,859 is received and disbursed as illustrated.

Trip to Rangitoto to celebrate the opening of roads on the island, 1930. *Lackland photo. Devonport Borough Council*

Rangitoto tidal swimming pool erected by convict labour, 1935. *New Zealand Herald*

1929

January 2: Council decides to consider rating of Defence lands.

1930

March 13: Concern over Defence Department using Narrow Neck as an ammunition dump.

April 10: Question of relative worth of bridge and ferries raised—Mayor feels a bridge is not vital to progress. W.E.L. Napier offers £500 for a bridge fund.

June 16: Visit to Rangitoto by Board and Lands Department to oversee policy of shack colonies.

November 8: Minister of Defence inspects defence lands on the grounds that 1/11 of borough lands are unrateable because of use by Navy etc. Total value £137,000.

December 11: Council suggests grass seed collection as a means to help unemployed.

1931

January 3: Unemployed used to clean up Mt Victoria cemetery.

February 2: Government refuses to allow loan for unemployed to work on Melrose Park. Beginning of conflict over harbour bridge—Auckland Harbour Bridge Co. Ltd. having just been granted a charter.

June 25: Reduction in rates from 7d to 6¾d in pound. Decision to cut council salaries by 7 per cent, exempting first £2 per week in wages, or £100 in salary. Council decides to dispense with the positions of foreman of works, building and sanitary inspectors, inspections assistant and waterworks inspector and re-advertise new positions in at lower salary. Council to save £410 per year.

1932

March 16: Council set up a committee to deal with the problems of unemployment relief.

August 4: The old power house to be offered for sale, the premises at present being used by the Devonport Welfare League.

August 10: The Domain Board proposes to proceed with a planting scheme for Mt. Victoria, using native trees.

October: More concern about Lake Pupuke falling one foot per year—water level down 12 feet in the last 20 years.

November 24: Mayor Meikle travels to Wellington to discuss relief schemes. Question raised again of North head to become a reserve for Devonport. Permission for a motorbus to carry passengers to the summit of Rangitoto Island.

December 15: Government cuts the allocation of works and wages to unemployed.

1933

February 4: The Board decides to pursue the Waitakere water scheme proposed by the Auckland City Council. Meanwhile the Council is forced to aerate the water supply from Lake Pupuke to make it drinkable.

March 16: Suggestion from the Health Department that drinking water be boiled. Relief workers propose a candidate for election although voting by property-holders alone.

March 23: Devonport decides against amalgamation with other North Shore boroughs.

April 6: Devonport calls for tenders for a water purification plant.

May 25: Question raised over treatment of relief workers by the Council.

July 6: Suggestion of using prison labour instead of relief workers on the No. 5 Relief Scheme of clearing weeds on Rangitoto.

July 20: Conflict between the tennis club and Domain Board over Sunday sport—the latter feels it is encroachment of continental ideas. James Mays dies.

September 19: Council opposes idea of a Milk Supply Control Board as interference with the laws of supply and demand. The welfare depot at the old power house is supplying 174 relief workers with firewood, vegetables, meat etc.

October: The Council becomes uneasy over supply of water from Auckland City Council despite Birkenhead's and Takapuna's acceptance. Turns to the Waikato Water Supply Co. or scheme from upper Wairau creek.

October 26: Council decides to ask Auckland City Council to put together a meeting about unemployment relief. Receives £40 from Auckland Metropolitan Unemployment Relief Committee for immediate relief purposes—315 men on relief work. Council blocks the North Shore Mayors' move to buy water from Auckland City Council.

October 31: Move to clean up the harbour with support from the Harbour Board.

1934

January 26: Moves to establish a Metropolitan Water Authority.

February 22: Council refuses to support a comprehensive drainage scheme for the area, saying the present one is sufficient.

March 22: Gun from Boer War is buried on Mt Victoria.

April 19: Decision by North Shore boroughs not to pursue amalgamation. Council's finances improved—£24,592 spent on relief.

May 17: Council buys a pistol to destroy dogs rather than use prussic acid.

1935

Labour Party involved in local elections.

May 2: Cr Aldridge wants an account of how relief money from the Unemployment Relief Board has been spent. A.W. Simpson accuses Council of using the system to get cheap labour. Complaints over treatment of Rangitoto Island.

July 5: Plans submitted for municipal buildings. The Mayor states that Council could have done better without unemployment relief workers as they were not healthy enough.

July 19: Council objects to the forced removal of 100 unemployed men to Hobsonville air base.

July 26: Council raises rates despite a decision to levy only on 75 per cent of Government valuation. The question of a harbour bridge raised once more.

September 20: Devonport withdraws from the Auckland Provincial Water Bill.

September 26: Council decides to inaugurate a subsidised system of superannuation for employees. Football grounds added at Stanley Bay. Council decides to take "straw vote" of the 2200 ratepayers for a town hall.

October 25: Council decides to ask the Unemployment Board to reconsider its decision not to subsidise the new town hall construction.

November 2: Protest meeting against cutting up Narrow Neck sections for houses. Decision to form Vauxhall Ratepayers Association.

November 29: The Devonport Unemployed Association requests from Council a subsidy of wages for men employed on the stone crusher—6d per hour.

December 12: Council decides to employ eight part-time relief workers for two weeks before Christmas. Bust of Seddon obtained—suggested one of Savage should also be acquired.

December 19: Council decides to instal seven sodium vapour lamps—three on Windsor Reserve, two at Cheltenham, one at Stanley Point and one at Narrow Neck.

1936

January 11: First suggestion of a tunnel under the harbour to Devonport.

February 2: Council becomes concerned about overcrowding in Buchanan Street, four families to one section.

April 2: Council restores all salary and wage cuts to Borough employees.

May 2: Ratepayers reject loan proposals for a new kiosk and town hall.

June 7: Council delays selling of its Narrow Neck sections in view of the Government's new housing policy.

July 19: A woman injured by falling stones from Council quarry is awarded £369 damages.

September 26: First North Shore state house tenants installed at 27 Niccol Avenue.

Novembr 10: New sodium vapour lamps inaugurated—first in Australasia. Thirty-four out of seventy-four subsidised workers Council employs are laid off with the ending of the Government's No. 13 scheme. Council accused of using the scheme to place thirty permanent employees on a subsidy basis.

November 14: Post Office to be moved to east side of Victoria Road.

November 17: The Takapuna Jockey Club proposes to hand over sixty-nine acres of land to Council.

1937

January 4: The Minister of Lands, Frank Langstone, views baches on Rangitoto Island and orders their removal. Rangitoto Island Protection League is formed in protest.

March 26: Bach owners on Rangitoto Island given twenty years to evacuate.

May 27: Brown's Island chosen for main drainage scheme for Auckland.

August 19: Housing survey report follows 2816 inspections. Overcrowding of 134 persons on Calliope Road—118 dwellings in Vauxhall Road found to be totally unfit to live in.

December 2: Council receives permission to act on the results of the housing survey—sanitary inspector to investigate cases of overcrowding.

1938

July 23: The old Flagstaff Hotel which was moved to the back of the Esplanade for servants' quarters is demolished.

July 28: Council contributes £22 towards the cost of a municipal airport survey.

September 8: Naval ammunition is no longer to be kept in the Borough.

September 22: The Auckland Harbour Board makes a suggestion for a boat harbour in Ngataringa Bay.

December 8: Council makes yet another proposal for a £12,000 loan for municipal buildings, public library, Plunket rooms and women's rest room.

December 22: Council is opposed to the proposal by the Takapuna Borough Council for a commission of inquiry into North Shore water supply.

1939

January 28: Criticism of a councillor's dress is made—he wore a "gay cherry blazer adorned with badges". Council congratulates Mr G. Ewington, who had voluntarily attended Council meetings for twelve years.

February 9: Classes held at Narrow Neck at the Northern Military District School of Instruction, showing people what to do in case of a gas attack.

February 18: Takapuna Jockey Club hands over racecourse and £800 to Council.

May 11: Council formally retires an old Council horse with "feet trouble".

June 1: Rat Week declared—free poison.

July 6: A Councillor expresses concern over the effect of a double unit state house on the amenities of Hamana Street. Decision that a Centennial memorial would be the upgrading of Cheltenham Beach bathing sheds.

July 19: Criticisms are made of the North Shore drainage outfall—pure sewage is being discharged off Narrow Neck.

September 16: The Government asks all bodies to desist soliciting for funds for war projects.

September 25: Rangitoto Island's main wharf and western and southern portions closed to the public.

October 3: Evacuation of bach owners on Rangitoto takes place.

December 1: Work is postponed on Cheltenham Beach because of the war. Devonport residents start to protest over the quality of water in the borough—people begin taking water from the Church Street well.

1940

January 1: The Mayor of Takapuna and some councillors "invade" Devonport to hold a public protest meeting over the quality of the water supply.

February 23: Achilles and Ajax Streets are named after the Battle of the River Plate.

May 16: The Council has town planning "explained" to it by a representative of the Internal Affairs Department.

June 4: The names of Devonport men and next-of-kin who are leaving in the 3rd Echelon are taken by Council for the Patriotic Committee. Council also takes the names of those willing to take allied refugee children.

July 25: The first New Zealand flag to be flown in occupied territory in the Great War is placed in the care of the Council by the Devonport School Committee. It was hoisted on to the wireless mast in Apia, Samoa, with the expeditionary force, August 1914.

August 8: Civic social and presentation for Devonport men of the 3rd Echelon going overseas.

August 26: Devonport seen as a danger zone if batteries go into action.

November 28: Council decides to form a Home Guard—recruiting at old Council Chambers.

December 9: First parade of the Home Guard.

December 12: Decision to buy 5000 gallons of water per day from Auckland City Council because of supply crisis. Thousands of dead fish in Lake Pupuke.

1941

January 23: Fire on Mt Victoria—ten years of tree planting lost.

February 15: Trial city-wide blackout.

October 2: Mayor R.G. May commented on the lack of interest in patriotic matters in Devonport. Council[1] decides to plant 350,000 onions, 100,000 to be planted in

an experimental plot in Alison Park.

October 30: Rehabilitation Committee for returning soldiers established.

1942

January 22: Trenches for 500 dug in Devonport. Council to dig trenches for the elderly.

February 5: Obsolete guns removed from reserves. Two guns on Windsor Reserve to be dismantled.

February 27: Meeting of concerned Devonport women at Methodist Hall to discuss air-raid shelters and slit trenches. Devonport considered to be a very real target. Confusion over evacuation plans.

March 5: Council makes arrangements to give protection to Emergency Protection Scheme workers crossing harbour by ferry.

March 11: All shops to close at 6pm on late nights as part of emergency regulations. Hairdressers and tobacconists exempted.

April 2: Plans for evacuation of women and children put before Council.

October 10: New water supply from Waitakeres is connected.

1943

January 29: Council considers plans for rehabilitation of returned servicemen after the war, being prepared to use men on the roads etc. at a cost of up to £100,000.

December 24: Ban on Rangitoto Island lifted.

1944

September 7: Council decides to see if it can re-light sodium vapour lamps turned off during the blackout.

September 28: Deputation to Council protesting the closing of Patuone Place for military needs. Two muzzle-loading cannons on Windsor Reserve for forty years given to the Naval base.

October 12: Council asks for the removal of the Narrow Neck military camp.

1945

August 15: Council requests citizens to sound sirens and show bunting immediately after

The former Post Office building in Victoria Rd being prepared for the Devonport Borough Council, 1940. *Auckland Star*

announcement of peace. A service of thanksgiving to be held in front of Council Chambers. A proclamation of community singing, band programmes and dancing in the square is given.

October 4: Council gives permission for films to be shown on Christmas Day—provided Council vets films.

1946

February 13: Large fire on Mt Victoria—four-fifths burnt.

May 3: Traffic Department takes permanent responsibility for traffic control.

June 6: Council tries to get Narrow Neck military camp for transit housing.

October 3: New by-law to control bathing costumes.

October 17: The Director-General of Health orders the Hospital Board to take over the military hospital at Narrow Neck for urgent cases.

October 23: Wrens demobbed—question of future of hostel buildings on Mt Victoria—Council refuses to allow buildings to remain.

October 26: Request for Narrow Neck camp turned down.

1947

March 21: Complaints to Rangitoto Island Board concerning the encroachment of pines on the island.

April 29: Council approves a five-year scheme for transit housing on Mt Victoria.

August 7: Council is given a demonstration of "vehicle activated traffic lights". Council contributes £36 to the rebuilding of the Guildhall in London.

September 2: Council participates in a joint

borough petition for a general hospital. Applications for transit housing reveal appalling housing conditions in Devonport.

September 18: First units on Mt Victoria occupied.

September 25: Member of Auckland Metropolitan Planning Association explains to Council plans for Devonport including multi-unit housing on slopes of Mt Victoria to house up to 10,000.

October 23: North Island schools closed because of poliomyelitis.

1948

January 12: Criticism of depredations by animals on Rangitoto.

March 1: Schools re-open. Harbour waters unsafe and people advised not to bathe. Takapuna decides to withdraw from the North Shore Borough Association.

June 24: Council considers the installation of "electronic" traffic signals on the corners of Lake and Albert Roads.

June 30: Proposal of a tip at Ngataringa Bay off Lake Road.

December 17: Band rotunda dismantled—kauri and totara foundations removed. Council intends to replace it with a soundshell.

1949

May 5: Council objects to communists holding street meetings.

August 3: Takapuna refuses to consider amalgamation.

1950

March 29: Protests at live gun practice at Narrow Neck—the first since the war.

April 22: First woman councillor, elected in 1947, dies.

1951

January 25: Council protests lack of representation on Harbour Bridge committee.

February 19: Council congratulates itself on removing all exotic trees from Rangitoto.

April 24: The four North Shore boroughs agree in principle to a North Shore Drainage Board.

The Royal car leaving Devonport Naval Base following the ceremonial parade and presentation of colours, 24 December 1953. *Alexander Turnbull Library*

May 3: Council offers to provide guards and patrols to protect military and naval installations in the borough during absence of military due to maritime strike.

1952

July 18: Twenty Norfolk pines to be planted on Lake Road on Arbor Day as part of a war memorial.

December 12: Council approves a scheme for naval housing at old brick works, Ngataringa Bay.

1953

March 26: Mass meeting in Windsor Reserve to protest delays on the harbour bridge.

May 15: Local bodies agree to share the cost of looking after Rangitoto.

May 28: Saluting battery installed on Mt Victoria.

October 28: Devonport tip to be controlled.

December 16: Council instructs the ranger to warn swimmers who are indecently attired in "hippy type" bathing costumes.

December 26: The Queen visits Devonport.

1954

January 15: Council decides to consider composting all organic refuse.

January 30: Timber from old Borough Council Chambers to be sold—rimu, kauri, oregon and jarrah.

February 4: Minister of Crown Lands rules that all bach owners have to be off Rangitoto by 1957.

February 17: Water shortage. Decision to mix Lake Pupuke water attracts complaints.

February 26: Devonport Library is taken over

by the Council in conjunction with the National Library Service.

March 21: New signal station completed on Mt Victoria—old tower served 109 years.

June: Council shows film it commissioned of the Queen's visit at Victoria Theatre.

August 26: Council commissions a mural for new Plunket rooms by Mrs Joan Stevens.

September 3: Devonport residents sign a petition for the return of £4000 lost revenue because of naval base.

September 16: Devonport centre opens.

November 2: Council decides to join the Auckland Regional Planning Authority.

November 22: Takapuna notifies Devonport of its intention to take under Public Works Act 6½ acres of land owned by the Council on the edge of Lake Pupuke.

December 21: Council decides to contribute £210 annually for the next ten years to the War Memorial.

1955

February 24: Council decides to build six old-age pensioner flats on Alison Park.

May 23: Council proposes a £200,000 loan—poll demanded by ratepayers at a cost of £500.

July: The Government plans to quarry Rangitoto.

December: Council decides to urge the Auckland Harbour Board to reclaim 300 acres of Ngataringa Bay. Council installs 150 parking meters.

1956

February 4: New band rotunda erected on the site of the old fountain. Designed by A.T. Griffiths, Borough engineer, who said 'I tried to design something ornamental but with a musical atmosphere'. Rail represents bars of music with 'God Save the Queen' in metal notation.

May 21: North Shore Hospital is begun.

May 30: Council employees join with army and police to search for several hundred detonators scattered on and around Cheltenham Beach.

August 29: Council makes application for loan for six pensioner flats.

September 19: Council abolishes party tickets for municipal elections.

November 30: Devonport declines to become involved in suggestions for amalgamation.

December 18: Council decides to build its first pensioner flats on Handley Avenue. People living on Rangitoto on 1 April 1955 are given a lifetime lease.

1957

February 23: Council decides to revert to its old policy of planting trees where possible.

May 2: Devonport Ratepayers Association suggests the building of a town hall out over the sea.

June 21: Minister of Works says he will not force Devonport Borough Council to give up land adjacent to Lake Pupuke.

September 25: Decision to have old Stanley Bay wharf demolished.

October 30: Council first to become a corporate member of the New Zealand Historic Places Trust.

November 6: Council seeks authority to have sections adjoining Devonport Domain on King Edward Parade used for high-density housing.

November 21: Council rescinds decision to support fluoridation of the city's water supply.

1958

February 5: Council considers philosophical implications for beach chairs on Cheltenham Beach—question of individual rights over common access.

February 25: Sunday movies are approved in order to stop hooliganism. Churches protest.

April 28: Old mast on Mt Victoria re-erected on Windsor Reserve.

June 20: Chamber of Commerce pushing for amalgamation of four boroughs despite strong protests from councils. Council workmen uncover a skeleton on King Edward Parade; one had been found

Parking meters were ignored when they were first introduced in 1956. A sign (*inset*) was set up to remind parkers of their obligations. *R. Simpson*

A 1954 photograph of the community building. *New Zealand Herald*

A CHRONOLOGY OF THE BOROUGH COUNCIL 155

An aerial view of Devonport in 1965. *White's Aviation*

previously—suggestions of a Maori battlefield. Letters received commending Sunday movies from New Zealand Rationalist Association. Cr A.W. Ferguson wants ensign flag raised and lowered each day—Mayor not prepared to waste Council employee's time. Councillor Wouldes complains of difficulties of acorns on footpaths.

1959
January 28: Three houses removed from Domain Land.
March 25: Deputation of residents on bylaw 20 which limits number of cats and dogs per household. Mayor considers whether possible to recommend birching of vandals.

1962
October 31: Residents suggest Devonport is declining—they want 'new blood' on the Council.
November 9: Council told they will have to prove Devonport Domain unsuitable for recreation before it can be taken for high-rise housing.
December 13: Debate over the Queen's visit—question whether to decorate the borough or not.

1963
January: Mayor R.S. Stevens denies a rift with Takapuna.
February 6: Council considers plans for Narrow Neck beach as a motor camp.
May 1: Decision to close the transit camp at Narrow Neck.
May 23: Council applies for a £10,000 rates loss per year. Decision to sell 6½ acres around Lake Pupuke for £25,000. Council accepts plans by the Automobile Association for the development of a high-class hotel at Narrow Neck.
May 29: One hundred signatures on a petition against a motor camp, hotel or skating rink at Narrow Neck. Navy authorised to buy houses on Calliope Road between Spring Street and Stanley Bay wharf—of the thirty-seven, eight are already owned by the navy.

September 4: The Government refuses to accept the heaviness of Devonport's defence burden.
September 13: Poor attendances at the Festival of Arts puts its future in doubt.
October 1: The Takapuna Lions Cub proposes a miniature railway on Windsor Reserve—Council in favour.
October 23: Petition of 100 signatures against the Railway.
October 24: Waitemata Golf Club to be built.
October 30: Threat to revive Devonport Ratepayers Association in recess since 1961, if Council continues to hold discussions in committee.
November 27: Council approves the miniature railway in principle but discusses a funicular railway because the ratepayers do not like the former idea.

1964
March 4: Residents irate about a Council decision to site a rubbish tip at Ngataringa Bay.
August 27: Council to ask residents to form a committee to consider proposals for a swimming pool, stage or soundshell for Windsor Reserve.
September 2: Council sets up a committee to consider three 12-storey blocks of flats containing 100 units for the waterfront on Torpedo Bay.
October 21: Council decides to ask the Minister of Lands whether it can use land on Devonport Domain for high-rise housing.
December 22: Further criticism of the state of the roads.

1965
March: Firm of architects engaged by the Council at a cost of £100 to prepare a plan for Windsor Reserve. To have a paddling pool, sound shell, dressing sheds and seafood restaurant.
April 28: The Minister of Lands refuses to allow flats on part of the Domain.
August 24: Council sends demands for 1d in arrears in rates to two dead sisters.

August 25: Council supports idea of a causeway between Takapuna, Bayswater and Devonport.

1966
April 21: Council gives approval for recreation plan for Windsor Reserve.
July 19: Council proposes housing on terraces of Alison Park—says too many reserves.
November 22: Council attempts to acquire North Head for high-density housing.

1967
February 9: Devonport, Northcote and East Coast Bays vote against proposals for the creation of North Shore city.
March 12: Town Planning approval (Appeal Board) given to the subdivision of Alison Park.
April 27: Council divided over the question of putting a miniature golf course on Woodall Park.
June 29: Cruelty to council sheep on Mt Victoria reported.
October 10: Time capsule found on the site of the Auckland Savings Bank building. Council loses control of Rangitoto to Hauraki Maritime Park Board.

1968
February 8: Pensioner flats plan for Fraser Road revived. Threat to sack Council over recreation plan for Windsor Reserve. Public meeting held.
April 23: Council proposes to prepare an enabling bill for Parliament to allow it to lease ⅝ acre of the reserve for proposed development. Mayor argues that it would allow Council to hold the rates.
April 23: Last official inspection of Rangitoto by the Rangitoto Island Domain Board.
June 1: Freedom of Devonport given to the navy.
June 20: Council considers taking six men for unemployment relief.
July 18: Causeway between Devonport and Takapuna included in regional plan. Two organisations, D.R. and R.A. and Windsor Reserve Protection Society to oppose the bill.

August 13: Devonport first to have a late-night Thursday.
August 27: Army advises Council it is willing to relinquish use of North Head—summit to be retained for the navy and three acres at southern end of Cheltenham.
September 10: Four women standing for Council. Devonport Ratepayers Association backs idea of high-density housing, upgrading Borough and developing Ngataringa Bay—as well as retaining Windsor Reserve.
September 24: Auckland Harbour Board approves a joint venture of £1.5 million with Devonport Borough Council to reclaim Ngataringa Bay for a marine-type residential subdivision.
November 5: Council decides the marineland is to go ahead—prevented by law that private gain could not be made out of a public domain.
November 20: Meeting of Auckland Harbour Board, Grohe Holdings Ltd, and Devonport Borough Council over Ngataringa Bay.
November 26: Navy stops Council high-rise scheme on North Head.

1969
February 23: Council decides it will not open committee meetings to the public—it was not in the public interest—and every Councillor would be required to attend all meetings.
March 11: $64,000 extensions for library complex.
April 5: Tender let for 12 old-age pensioner flats in Fraser Road.
May 6: Proposal made to Council for a restaurant on Mt Victoria.
June 22: Subdivision between Alison Park and Empire Road to be auctioned.
June 24: Businessmen's Association continues to support marina plan.
July 22: Auckland Harbour Board approves $5 million marina, 370 sections, each on 1/5 acre, jetty and water access, with public marina and boat ramps. Auckland Regional Authority comes out in support of marina.

August: Beginning of organised protest on grounds of conservation, access, public access to information and the right of consultation.

September 4: Any pages dealing with Ngataringa Bay in Council minutes are deleted.

September 23: Agreement reached for joint responsibility for the Ngataringa Bay scheme between Auckland Harbour Board and Devonport Borough Council. Bill to be drafted empowering them to reclaim 24 acres. Harbour bed and channel to remain vested in Devonport Borough Council.

September 30: The Institute of Surveyors oppose the scheme, until overall scheme for the Waitemata comes under the Town and Country Planning Act.

September 18: Friends of the Devon Isles Marine Department, Ngataringa Bay, established.

December 16: Three architecture students design a restaurant for Mt Victoria and a gondola cable-car from Devonport Wharf.

1970

February 16: Council voices its disappointment over the route the Queen was to take up Calliope Road.

February 24: Vauxhall School 50th jubilee celebrations.

March 24: Second marineland scheme turned down.

March 28: Jaycees propose a concrete block fort for Windsor Reserve.

May 7: Members of Local Government Commission visit Ngataringa Bay.

May 12: Devonport School 100th jubilee.

May 21: Notice of first review of district scheme. Three residential zones promised. Council decides no restricted films on Sundays.

June 22: Council calls for the removal of the army from North Head so the Maritime Park Board can operate there. Council to prepare a development plan for Mt Victoria.

June 23: Council gives the beginning of its approval for high-rise flats on King Edward Parade.

June 25: Council suggests Takapuna City takes over O'Neill's Point Cemetery.

July 16: Council informed the navy will stay until 1975.

July 22: Australian Ombudsman Association tries to take legal action against North Shore Ferries to stop 'ferry jumping'. Council sides with the commuters' right to jump.

July 30: Devonport Borough Planning Group plan first meeting.

September 24: Mt Victoria trees planted two years previously need clearing and stock kept out.

October 1: Council to pass by-law preventing boats in Windsor Reserve.

October 2: Auckland Harbour Board and Borough Council Empowering Bill reported back to Parliament after a year.

October 22: Jonathan Hunt states opposition to Ngataringa Bay scheme.

November 30: North Shore Labour Youth meeting against Bay.

December 16: Auckland Museum states opposition to the scheme.

1971

January 28: Council receives largest number of objections to a reviewed district scheme—largest number from Devonport Planning Association.

May 26: Mayor Jackson threatens the suspension of Councillors if any committee information is leaked. Council decides to press for causeway access to the Borough.

November 20: After 25 years the Ministry of Transport finds that Council is acting illegally in setting parking aside for Council staff.

November 23: Council proposes to buy the old State Theatre for youth groups.

1972

May 25: Council permits "R" movies on Sundays—Methodists object to the certain flood of pornography. Mayor proposes that all money for roads be spent on a causeway.

June 21: Rates up 21 per cent—30 per cent from increased levies.

August 15: Devonport School demolished.

August 19: Council considers using half-acre of Devonport Domain for a carpark for North Shore Rugby Club.

August 22: Reviewed district scheme approved.

December 13-14: Two public meetings held re Ngataringa Bay.

1973

January 27: Eighty people ejected from Council meeting after fuss when Mayor says Councillors will not attend public meetings. Public meeting of 800 give a vote of no confidence in Council.

January 26: Hugh Watt visits Ngataringa Bay and is concerned about scheme.

February 6: Councillors to speak on reasons for support for Ngataringa Bay. Council votes eight to two for bay reclamation.

February 22: Councillors Pritchard and W.D. Titchener are excluded from Ngataringa Bay Improvement Association meeting.

February 27: Devonport Planning Association attacks tip in Ngataringa Bay.

Marcy 20: Sixty per cent of Devonport houses qualify for home improvement loans.

March 27: Vauxhall Tennis Club to build a new clubhouse. Dromgoole threatens to turn ferry service over to the Auckland Regional Authority. Council concerned that Authority will stop the service or increase transport levies.

April 30: Parliamentary Local Bills Committee to hear 24 submissions over Empowering Act.

May 1: Possible subpoena on secret report concerning Ngataringa Bay to Auckland Regional Authority. Developer tells Local Bills Committee he would seek compensation if Ngataringa Bay scheme dropped. Council agrees to try a one-way system in Church Street.

May 22: Council extends developer's licence for two years. Councillor Pritchard wants it renegotiated. Auckland Regional Authority says it will not confirm Bay plan until the Waitemata Harbour Plan study completed.

October 23: Council to provide bins for glass recycling collections. Councillor Titchener tries to stop the Council going into committee over report by Ngataringa Bay sub-committee.

November 19: Council dismisses the idea of a restaurant and viewing tower on Mt Victoria.

1974

February 21: Council reaffirms that Ngataringa Bay will be transferred as freehold.

March 12: Council embarks on a photographic record of Devonport.

April 20: A New Zealand company is formed to buy out the US interest in Ngataringa Bay.

May 28: New scheme for Bay put before Council. Council tries to give itself control over building design, appearance and maintenance. Council sidesteps issue of planning approval for the scheme and the public's right to object. Mt Victoria cemetery to be formally closed to allow Council to work on it under the Burial and Cremation Act 1964.

June 14: Council plans a register of buildings. Councillor Pritchard pushes for open committee meetings, supported by Councillor Worrall.

July 9: Draft scheme plan for Ngataringa Bay approved in principle by Council.

July 23: Council to plant flowering shrubs on Devonport Domain. Anne Salmond says Ngataringa Bay development would be social suicide.

October 15: Council presented with a petition asking them to protest the taking of houses for Ngataringa Bay. Developer says he will press on with the Ngataringa Bay scheme despite the new Council being overwhelmingly against it.

November 19: Council decides to divulge information on Ngataringa Bay.

November 26: Council discusses its legal dilemma if it tries to rescind previous agreements with developer.

November 29: Auckland Regional Authority Planning Committee comes out against the Ngataringa Bay plan. Report by Malcolm Latham for Auckland Regional Authority revealed.

December 12: Some Devonport land values up 331 per cent.

1975

January 8: Extension of time for environmental report made.

January 23: Council believes developer had no right to submit an environmental impact report directly to the Commissioner for the Environment.

February 20: Council plans to raise $297,000 water loan.

April 22: Historic olive trees at Vauxhall Road school to get a face lift.

May 1: A.N. Sexton, tree consultant, suggests the removal of trees on Windsor Reserve. Council supports United Arts Enterprises' acquisition of the old State Theatre.

October 30: All Councils forced to hold open meetings under the Public Bodies Meetings Amendment Act.

December 16: Duders Beach to be kept for swimmers only.

1976

February 16: Mayor accuses Councillor S. Mills of using Council to put forward political views on nuclear warships.

February 29: Margaret Fraser objects to a playcentre on Woodall Park at Narrow Neck.

March 1: Bob Pope wants Council to resign for a clearer mandate over compensation court action.

A borough resident drops off recyclable material at the Devonport Borough Council's landfill site. *Ron Johnson, Devonport Borough Council*

March 23: Council decides to support Lake Road as the best access corridor.

July 20: Town Planning Committee recommends refusal of a supermarket near gasworks.

July 29: Council asks for Government assurance that no nuclear ships will berth at Devonport base.

September 2: Auckland Regional Authority backs a small experimental rubbish recycling scheme promoted by Council and four community groups.

September 30: Paul Titchener wants two 64 pound guns at navy base returned to Windsor Reserve. Council declines but declares Council ownership.

October 21: Playcentre to be at Band headquarters on Mt Victoria.

October 27: Council sends letter of protest about nuclear ships to Government.

December 2: Plans to preserve old pumphouse on Stanley Bay.

December 6: Plans to develop retail space in Victoria Road by using backs of shops.

December 16: Rock concert to be held on Windsor Reserve.

1977

February 15: Recycling demonstration on Windsor Reserve.

March 1: Council installs arch on King Edward Parade with funds from the Watson bequest—designed by R.H. Keely. Protests that Council selling compost bins will encroach on private enterprise.

March 8: Ngataringa Bay hearings set for September 12.

March 29: Tip recycling facilities opened.

May 12: Devonport Museum Society asks Council to underwrite lease for house on 26 Anne Street for $500.

May 23: Council calls special meeting to discuss ferries.

June 21: Defence Ministry approves of "Wrennery", Elizabeth House, to go in historic buildings listing.

August 18: Important savings being made in recycling of steel.

September 8: Voting for elections to be held over eleven days.

September 29: Council favours North Shore local bodies sharing the cost of a sub-regional recreation complex.

October 4: Council elections. New budgeting system instigated by Town Clerk.

October 25: Justice Perry reserves opinion about Ngataringa Bay.

November 29: Museum to move to Parish Hall, which is to be moved to depot site.

December 19: Tip filling too fast—decision to confine it to Devonport residents.

1978

March 28: Council threatens to refer North Shore Ferries to the Transport Licensing Authority for second time in one year.

May 2: Council ruled liable in Ngataringa Bay case. North Shore Ferries to approach Council for a subsidy.

May 16: Councillors found not to be personally liable for Ngataringa Bay.

May 28: Vince Terrine, Bamboo Tower Society, requests to build a tower on Mt Victoria.

June 1: Council decides to appeal against Ngataringa Bay decision.

September 13: Ngataringa Bay developer claims $3m damages.

October 10: Under the new Reserves Act management plans are required for Council reserves.

October 19: Walkway and tree planting on strip of reserve running out to Ngataringa Bay from Patuone and Mozley Avenues. Plan to upgrade clay store.

November 30: Dogs permitted on beaches before 9am and after 6pm.

1979

April 3: Council offers $20,000 subsidy to North Shore Ferries—in return they want separate company of both Council and company representatives to run the service.

April 12: Council appeals against Ngataringa Bay decision fails.

April 19: Council offers house for the IHC in Seabreeze Road.

May 3: Council considers going to the Privy Council over Ngataringa Bay.

June 6: Council moves away from a flat rate on land values to user pays principle.

June 11: House sales steady despite prospect of a large compensation claim.

July 24: Council to negotiate with Auckland Harbour Board for extension of tenure of tip site.

July 26: Council cleans reservoir on Mt Victoria.

August 7: Waitemata Golf Club wants to demolish old Takapuna Jockey Club building and construct a new building. Old barracks on Mt Victoria to be developed. Council encountering problems with plastics at tip.

August 28: Council to offer house at 22 Seabreeze Road to Laotian family.

September 11: Devonport water systems found to need upgrading.

October 9: Ferry company rejects offer of subsidy from Council.

October 23: Mayor and Cr Pritchard take ferry/bus problem to Wellington.

October 31: meeting to discuss naval wharf.

November 21: Council seeks advice in relation to $3.6m damages claim from developer. Council establishes questions for environmental impact report about a nuclear wharf.

1980

February 26: Council refuses nude beaches.

March 25: Central Government recognises importance of Council's recycling scheme.

March 27: Council approves navy plans for a 'nuclear biological chemical school' (fire fighting school) at Ngataringa Bay.

May 15: Ngataringa Bay compensation set at $750,000.

May 20: Rates to rise—only half due to Ngataringa Bay. No land sales etc.

June 17: W.D. Titchener appointed Mayor.

June 24: Ngataringa Bay Society drafts petition asking for alternative ways to pay the claim. Society includes Council members, Devonport Action Group, Ngataringa Bay Improvement Society and Devonport Ratepayers.

July 1: Two phoenix palms removed from Windsor Reserve.

July 7: Devonport Action Group decide to boycott Council sub-committee set up to find ways of raising finance other than through rates.

August 15: Study to take place on future of dockyard.

September 9: Incorporated society established to consider Ngataringa Bay. Council sub-committees too restricted.

September 22: Council declares itself a nuclear-free zone.

North Head demonstration during arrival of USS *Texas*, 2 August 1983. *John Miller*

November 25: Council to call for the repeal of the Ngataringa Bay Empowering Act.

December 1: Arthur Griffiths, engineer with the Council from 1921-1968, dies.

December: Auckland Regional Authority refuses to help Council with payment of compensation.

1981

January 13: Auckland Harbour Board refuses to help Council in payments.

March 3: Urban Transport Act to be examined.

March 21: Devonport Festival art auction raises $10,000.

June 25: Council questions navy's sports complex plan.

August 4: Suggestions that old Devonport fire station be pulled down.

1982

January 6: Navy wharf to proceed. Council given no assurance that it is not for nuclear ships.

March 9: Trees felled on North Head—Council protests.

April 20: Devonport plans $1m loan for road work.

April 28: Increasing problem of plastics at tip.

June 26: Ratepayers attack Council spending in a leaflet.

July 7: Knife attack on Mayor.

October 12: Council applies for $250,000 loan for sewerage system—guarantee of 0.06 cents in the dollar for land value on all rateable property.

November 30: Claystore may become art centre—at present Salvation Army using top floor for work scheme.

A young Devonportian looks across to Auckland from beneath the King Edward VII Coronation Memorial. *Chris Miller*

Office-holders and Councillors 1886-1986

MAYORS

M. NICCOL	1886-1890
E.W. ALISON	1890-1895
M. NICCOL	1895-1896
J.C. MACKY	1896-1901
M. NICCOL	1901-1902
E.W. ALISON	1902-1907
W. HANDLEY	1907-1915
A.M. PICKFORD	1915-1916
J. HENDERSON	1916-1919
H.S.W. KING	1919-1923
T. LAMONT	1923-1927
E. ALDRIDGE	1927-1930
J. HISLOP	1930-1931
J.F.W. MEIKLE	1931-1941
R.G. MAY	1941-1944
J.R. MILLER	1944-1950
C.F. WOODALL	1950-1959
F.S. STEVENS	1959-1965
J.H. SEEYLE	1965-1968
E. JACKSON	1968-1973
P.G. SHEEHAN	1973-1980
W.D. TITCHENER	1980-

COUNCILLORS

*MALCOLM NICCOL	1886
THOMAS JOHN DUDER	1886
JAMES MAYS	1886
EDWARD WILLIAM BURGESS	1886
*EWEN WILLIAM ALISON	1886
EDWARD BARTLEY	1886
HENRY PITTS	1886
RICHARD CAMERON	1886
WILLIAM PHILCOX	1886
WILLIAM HOILE BROWN	1886
ROBERT H. DUDER	1887
HEMI JEAN LE BAILLY	1889
JOSEPH GLENNY	1889
PHILLIP HAWE MASON	1889
WILLIAM BOND	1891
JOSEPH MACKY	1891
GEORGE LANKHAM	1891
FREDERICK JAMES HAMMOND	1892
WILLIAM AVENELL	1892
OLIVER MAYS	1892
SAMUEL COCHRANE MACKEY	1893
ROBERT WYNYARD	1893
EDMUND DUTTON	1894
JAMES CUTHBERTSON ENTRICAN	1895
ALEXANDER HARVEY	1895
JAMES DUNNING	1896
GEORGE HARVEY BROOKES	1896
ROBERT MITCHELL	1896
*WILLIAM HANDLEY	1896
GEORGE ANNEAR CREETH	1896
ROBERT LOGAN JR	1899
HENRY JOHN BAULF	1900
JOHN ATKINSON WALKER	1900
JOHN WILLIAM HARRISON	1901
FRANK ERNEST MASON	1901
WILLIAM JOHN WILLIMER PHILSON	1901

CHARLES PRIMROSE MURDOCH	1902		JOSEPH WOODALL	1915
CHARLES CRAVEN DACRE	1903		WALTER SAMUEL STONE	1915
GEORGE V. EDGCUMBE	1903		JOSEPH PATRICK WRIGHT	1915
JAMES BANNATYNE GRAHAM	1903		FREDERICK AUGUSTUS THOMPSON	1916
ERNEST GEORGE ROBERT FORD	1905		ISRAEL JOHN FLETCHER	1917
DUNCAN WILLIAM McLEAN	1905		WILLIAM PERRY TAYLOR	1918
WREFORD UPTON TUNEWELL	1905		SAMUEL WATKIN LUXFORD	1919
EDWARD JOHN OSBORNE	1905		THOMAS HENRY PALMER	1919
THOMAS WAKEHAM CRANCH	1907		GEORGE EDWARD VINCENT PEARCE	1919
ROBERT HENRY FROUDE	1907		WILLIAM ANDREW PILKINGTON	1919
GEORGE ARTHUR GRIBBEN	1907		ROBERT ARTHUR SPINLEY	1919
PATRICK WILLIAM McCULLUM	1907		ALFRED BARTLEY	1921
GEORGE McKENZIE	1907		*ERNEST HAWKINS LITTLE	1921
HENRY WILDING	1907		RALPH THOMAS MICHAELS	1921
THOMAS CONSIDINE	1909		CHARLES LANHAM STEVENSON	1921
WYNDHAM GRATTAN GUINNESS	1909		*ERNEST ALDRIDGE	1923
GEORGE WRIGHT RAVENHILL	1909		STEPHEN BOND	1923
JOHN TAYLOR	1909		*JOHN HISLOP	1923
JAMES KENDALL GASCOIGNE	1911		WILLIAM SCOTT CAMPBELL	1925
JOHN ALLEN	1911		FREDERICK JOSEPH ELLISDON	1925
LOCKIE GANNON	1911		ISRAEL MASSEY	1925
WILLIAM PARSONS	1911		WILLIAM ESMOND LENNOX NAPIER	1925
ARTHUR GILBERT QUARTLEY	1911		SAMUEL WALKER	1925
ALFRED JOHN TAPPER	1911		OLIVER WILBERT MARKS	1925
ADAM NIXON	1912		CHARLES MORGAN BROWNE	1927
ALICK MERRIOTT PICKFORD	1913		HENRY ARCHIBALD CAMPBELL	1927
JOHN GROOM WEBSTER	1913		TIMOTHY CARR ENRIGHT	1927
JOHN HENDERSON	1913		SIMON HENRY LYON	1927
JOSEPH KEW HARTY	1913		PATRICK JAMES SHEEHAN	1927
ARTHUR LLOYD	1913		THOMAS WALSH	1927
FREDERICK LOUIS ARMITAGE	1915		WILLIAM CASSELLS-BROWN	1929
WILLIAM KING HOWITT	1915		FRED TEMPEST EYRE	1929
THOMAS LAMONT	1915		GEORGE FALLA	1929
CHARLES JOSEPH SMITH	1915		JAMES CURTAYNE	1931

ALLEN SHREWSBURY PLAYER	1931	ROY PEARD HENRY MAYS	1953
GEORGE HARNETT	1931	ALGAR WALTON FERGUSON	1953
GEORGE DOUGLAS HARDY	1931	EDWIN JOHN ROBB	1953
COLIN FARQUHASSON	1931	CLAUDE WILLIAM BRASH	1956
ALFRED WILLIAM D. MEIKLEJOHN	1931	HENRY HUIA CAMP	1956
*HUBERT JOHN HUTCHINGS	1931	GORDON ERIC AMOS	1956
*WILLIAM FREDERICK MURDOCH		SYDNEY MATTHEW WOULDES	1958
MACLEAN	1933	WILLIAM EDWARD BARLOW	1959
*HUGH FERRY-WHEIR MEIKLE	1933	*JAMES DICKSON WATT	1959
*ANGUS MCDONALD	1935	*JOHN DOUGLAS BURNETT	1959
THOMAS CHARLES HOBBS-JONES	1935	MERVYN TOYNE BERNARD HARRIS	1959
SAMUEL SWANTON GREEN	1935	WILLIAM BANCROFT MASSEY	1962
ALEXANDER MACGREGOR	1938	*DESMOND CLIFFORD PARSONS	1962
THOMAS MASON	1938	RONALD HENRY WILCOX	1962
HARRY MORRIS	1938	RONALD THOMAS JACKA	1965
ALFRED WILSON JOUGHIN	1941	MARY JACKSON	1965
GORDON NOEL LLOYD KNIGHT	1941	ERIC ROY SUTHERLAND	1965
DAVID JOSEPH FREDERICK LANGLEY	1941	RODWELL ALFRED WEBB	1965
ARTHUR MASSEY	1941	PETER CARNAHAN	1968
PERCY CECIL BLENKARNE	1942	ALBERT JAMES HENDERSON	1968
JOHN DONALD GRAHAM DROUGHT	1944	NEIL HAMILTON HUME	1968
REGINALD NAPIER YATES	1944	*PATRICK GEORGE SHEEHAN	1968
JOHN WILLIAM LESLIE BUCHANAN	1947	GAVIN LYTTON ARMSTRONG	1971
CHRISTINA PILKINGTON	1947	PETER CHARLES NORRIS	1971
ALBERT ALFRED JARVIE	1947	*MICHAEL HERBERT PRITCHARD	1971
*EDWIN JACKSON	1949	*WRAY DAVIES TITCHENER	1971
MILTON GROSVENOR MABEE	1950	KAY NUI WORRALL	1974
RALPH OLIVER EAGLES	1950	GEOFFREY ALLAN LINDSAY AMOS	1974
CATHERINE MAUD RAINS	1950	*KELVIN CHARLES GRANT	1974
GORDON HOLM BISS	1950	ROBERT HERBERT SWANSON KEELY	1974
GEOFFREY MONKHOUSE CAMPLIN	1950	JOYCE ALWYN LOVETT	1974
ROBERT WILLIAM GEORGE SEAGER	1950	JOHN WILFRED MANNING	1974
*FREDERICK SEDGWICK STEVENS	1950	STEPHEN JAMES MILLS	1974
*HARRY ANDERSON	1950	CHRISTINE PATRICIA FRANTZEN	1977

WENDY HOLLYER	1977
ANN PATRICIA JOUGHIN	1977
EUSTACE EDGAR SUCKLING	1978
SYLVESTER JOHN PETER HENRICKSEN	1979
ALLAN GEORGE CAMERON	1980
MARGARET EDITH FRASER	1980
VIRGINIA JACQUELINE O. HORROCKS	1980
CAMERON TENISON MAINGAY	1980
ERNEST DAVID LINDSAY MARSDEN	1980
PATRICK JOHN SULLIVAN	1982
IAN LESLIE STUART BRADLEY	1983
ROBERT SINCLAIR MACDUFF	1983
THOMAS EDWIN SMITH	1983

The date represents the first declaration of office and the asterisk denotes Councillors who served for more than ten years as Councillor and/or as Mayor.

TOWN CLERKS

B. TANNER	1886-
S. DINSDALE	1886-1898
J.C. WEBSTER	1898-1910
J. WILSON	1910-1915
F. MORTIMER	1915-1918
J. WILSON	1918-1924
A.E. WILSON	1924-1958
D. MACLEAN	1958-1967
K.R. JOHNSON	1967-1974
J.L. McDERMOTT	1974-

BOROUGH ENGINEERS

VARIOUS CONSULTING ENGINEERS	1881-1922
A.T. GRIFFITHS	1922-1968
A.H. DENNIS	1969-1979
J.F. DEADY	1980-

Index